First World War
and Army of Occupation
War Diary
France, Belgium and Germany

7 DIVISION
Divisional Troops
Royal Army Veterinary Corps
12 Mobile Veterinary Section
15 September 1914 - 30 November 1917

WO95/1648/3

The Naval & Military Press Ltd
www.nmarchive.com
Published in association with The National Archives

Published by

The Naval & Military Press Ltd

Unit 10 Ridgewood Industrial Park,

Uckfield, East Sussex,

TN22 5QE England

Tel: +44 (0) 1825 749494

www.naval-military-press.com

www.nmarchive.com

This diary has been reprinted in facsimile from the original. Any imperfections are inevitably reproduced and the quality may fall short of modern type and cartographic standards.

Contents

Document type	Place/Title	Date From	Date To
Heading	WO95/1648/3		
Heading	7th Division Troops No.12 Mobile Vety Section Sep 1914-1917 Nov to Italy Dec 17		
Miscellaneous	7th Div A.V.C. No.12 Mobile Section Jan-Dec 1915		
Heading	7th Div 12/M.V.S 15.9-31.12.14 Jan 1919		
Heading	12/M.V.S		
War Diary	Woolwich	15/09/1914	16/09/1914
War Diary	Beaulieu Rd	16/09/1914	21/11/1914
War Diary	Ypres	01/11/1914	02/11/1914
War Diary	Poperinge	03/11/1914	07/11/1914
War Diary	Bailleul	08/11/1914	15/11/1914
War Diary	Sailly	16/11/1914	19/11/1914
War Diary	Croix Du Bac	20/11/1914	31/12/1914
Heading	7th Division No.12 Mobile Vety Section Vol I 1 Jan-28 Feb 1915		
War Diary	Croix Du Bac	11/01/1915	28/02/1915
Heading	7th Division 12th Mobile Vety Section Vol II 4-31.3.15		
War Diary	Croix Du Bac	04/03/1915	04/03/1915
War Diary	Blebutour	04/03/1915	08/03/1915
War Diary	Estaires	08/03/1915	27/03/1915
War Diary	Merville	29/03/1915	31/03/1915
War Diary	Croix Du Bac	01/03/1915	03/03/1915
War Diary	Blenbury Veins Berquin	04/03/1915	07/03/1915
War Diary	Estaires	08/03/1915	26/03/1915
War Diary	Merville	27/03/1915	31/03/1915
Heading	7th Division No.12 Mobile Vety Section Vol III 1-29.4.15		
War Diary	Merville	01/04/1915	30/04/1915
Heading	7th Division No.12 Mobile Vety Section Vol IV 1-31.5.15		
War Diary		01/05/1915	15/05/1915
War Diary	Estaires	16/05/1915	16/05/1915
War Diary	Bethune	18/05/1915	21/05/1915
War Diary	Lillers	23/05/1915	31/05/1915
Heading	7th Division No.12 Mobile Vety Section Vol V 1-30.6.15		
War Diary	Lillers	01/06/1915	03/06/1915
War Diary	Bethune	04/06/1915	30/06/1915
War Diary	Lillers	01/06/1915	03/06/1915
War Diary	Bethune	04/06/1915	30/06/1915
Heading	7th Division No 12 Mobile Vety Section Vol VI		
War Diary	Bethune	04/07/1915	04/07/1915
War Diary	Lillers	05/07/1915	29/07/1915
War Diary	Bethune	01/07/1915	03/07/1915
War Diary	Lillers	06/07/1915	31/07/1915
Heading	7th Division No 12 Mobile Vety Section Vol VII August 15		
War Diary	Lillers	03/08/1915	15/08/1915
War Diary	Pacaut	17/08/1915	31/08/1915
War Diary	Lillers	01/08/1915	16/08/1915

War Diary	Pacaut	18/08/1915	20/08/1915
War Diary	Bethune	21/08/1915	31/08/1915
Heading	7th Division No.12 Mobile Vety Section Vol VIII Sept 15		
War Diary	Bethune	05/09/1915	05/09/1915
War Diary	Fouquereil	06/09/1915	30/09/1915
Heading	7th Division No.12 Mobile Vety Section Vol IX Oct 15		
War Diary		03/10/1915	31/10/1915
Heading	7th Division No.12 Mob. Vety Sect Nov Vol X		
War Diary	Bethune	01/11/1915	30/11/1915
Heading	7th Div 12 Mob. Vet. Sec. Dec Vol XI		
War Diary		01/12/1915	31/12/1915
War Diary	Belloy	01/02/1916	29/02/1916
Heading	No.12 Mobile Vet. Section War Diary of Captain J.M Dawson AVC From 1st To 31st March 1916 Vol 13		
War Diary		01/03/1916	31/03/1916
Heading	No.12 Mobile Veterinary Section War Diary of Captain J.M. Dawson AVC From 1st To 30th April 1916 Vol 14		
War Diary		01/04/1916	30/04/1916
Heading	No.12 Mobile Veterinary Section War Diary of Captain J.M. Dawson A.V.C. From 1st To 31st May 1916 Vol 15		
War Diary	Merricourt	03/05/1916	31/05/1916
Miscellaneous	No.12 Mobile Veterinary Section War Diary of Captain J.M. Dawson AVC From 1st To 30th June 1916 Vol 16		
War Diary		02/06/1916	30/06/1916
Heading	12th Mobile Vet Section War Diary of Captain J.M. Dawson AVC From 1st To 31st July 1916 Vol 17		
War Diary		01/07/1916	31/07/1916
Heading	12 Mob Vet Section War Diary of Captain J.M. Dawson A.V.C. O/O 12 Mobile Section 7th Div From 1st To 31st Aug 1916 Vol 18		
War Diary		01/08/1916	31/08/1916
Heading	War Diary of Captain J.M. Dawson AVC 12 Mobile Section 7th Division From 1st September 1916 To 30th Sept 1916 Vol 19		
War Diary		01/09/1916	30/09/1916
Heading	War Diary of Captain J.M. Dawson A.V.C. O/C 12 Mobile Section 7th Division From 1st October 1916 To 31st October 1916 Vol 20		
War Diary		01/10/1916	31/10/1916
Heading	War Diary of Captain J.M. Dawson A.V.C. O/C.12 Mobile Vet Section 7th Division From 1st Nov 1916 To 30th Nov 1916 Vol 21		
War Diary		01/11/1916	30/11/1916
Heading	War Diary of Captain J.M. Dawson A.V.C. 12. Mobile Vety Section 7th Division From 1st To 31st Dec 1916 Vol 22		
War Diary		01/12/1916	31/12/1916
Heading	War Diary of Captain J.M. Dawson A.V.C. O/C 12 Mobile Section AVC 7th Division From 1st January 1917 To 31st January 1917 Vol 23		
War Diary		01/01/1917	31/01/1917

Heading	War Diary of Captain J.M. Dawson A.V.C. 12 Mobile Vety Section 7th Division From 1st February 1917 To 28th February 1917 Vol 24		
War Diary		01/02/1917	28/02/1917
Heading	War Diary of Captain J.M. Dawson A.V.C. O/C 12 Mobile Section 7th Division From 1st March 1917 To 31st March 1917 Vol 25		
War Diary		01/03/1917	31/03/1917
Heading	War Diary of Captain J.M. Dawson A.V.C. 12 Mobile Veterinary Section 7th Division From 1st April To 30th April 1917 Vol 26		
War Diary		01/04/1917	30/04/1917
Heading	War Diary of Captain J.M. Dawson A.V.C. O/C 12 Mobile Vety Section 7th Division 1917 May 1st To 31st Vol 27		
War Diary		01/05/1917	31/05/1917
Heading	War Diary of Captain J.M. Dawson A.V.C. O/C 12 Mobile Section AVC 7th Division From 1st June To 30th June 1917 Vol 28		
War Diary		01/06/1917	30/06/1917
Heading	War Diary of Captain J.M. Dawson A.V.C. 12 Mobile Veterinary Section 7th Division From 1st July To 31st July 1917 Vol 29		
War Diary		01/07/1917	31/07/1917
Heading	War Diary No 12 Mobile Vety Section Vol 37		
War Diary	Behagnies	01/08/1917	10/08/1917
War Diary	Bretencourt (Riviere)	11/08/1917	30/08/1917
Heading	War Diary 12th Mobile Veterinary Section September 1917 Vol 31		
War Diary	Reninghelst	01/09/1917	01/09/1917
War Diary	Steenvoorde	02/09/1917	03/09/1917
War Diary	Hondeghem	04/09/1917	13/09/1917
War Diary	Arques	14/09/1917	15/09/1917
War Diary	Wizernes	16/09/1917	28/09/1917
War Diary	Hondeghem	29/09/1917	29/09/1917
War Diary	Westoutre	30/09/1917	30/09/1917
Heading	War Diary 12 Mob Vety Section Vol 38		
War Diary	Westoutre	01/10/1917	01/10/1917
War Diary	La Clytte	02/10/1917	12/10/1917
War Diary	Berthen	13/10/1917	23/10/1917
War Diary	Westoutre	24/10/1917	29/10/1917
War Diary	Blaringhem	30/10/1917	31/10/1917
Heading	12 Mob Vety Section War Diary Volume No.39		
War Diary	Racquinghem	01/11/1917	13/11/1917
War Diary	Boyaval	14/11/1917	17/11/1917
War Diary	Wavrans	18/11/1917	19/11/1917
War Diary	Legnago	26/11/1917	26/11/1917
War Diary	Pojana	27/11/1917	27/11/1917
War Diary	Albettone	28/11/1917	30/11/1917

7TH DIVISION TROOPS

NO.12 MOBILE VETY SECTION

SEP 1914 - ~~JAN 1919~~ 1917 NOV

TO ITALY DEC '17

Index

SUBJECT.

7TH DIV.

No.	Contents.	Date.
	A.V.C.	
	No. 12 MOBILE SECTION	
	JAN. - DEC, 1915	

(56,425). Wt.24,741—161. 2000. 11/20. Gp.164. A.&E.W.

7th Div.

12/ M.V.S.

15·9 — 31·12·14

Jan 1919

12/M.V.S.

Instructions regarding War Diaries an… Summaries are contained in F. S. Regs., Part II. and the Staff Manual respectively. Title pages will be prepared in manuscript.

R DIARY
or
~~INTELLIGENCE SUMMARY~~ Sept. 1914

(Erase heading not required.)

Army Form C. 2118.

Hour, Date, Place	Summary of Events and Information	Remarks and references to Appendices
15.9.14. Woolwich	Personnel mobilised. Section is one short of War Establishment — no Cavalry Reservists available as batman so O.C. Records A.V.C. details one batman 'in lieu'.	During the period dealt with examination of Mob Store Table revealed deficiencies in Equipment which were likely to prove obstacles to the carrying out of the work of Section.
16/9/14 7-30am. Woolwich.	Entrained for Beaulieu to join 7th Division with Personnel. Orders from O.C. Depot. Letter from W.O.	Application made to W.O. for R.Q. Halters & Cattle Killer — noted that Table contains Flagpole & Crosspiece for Lamps but no provision for lamps.
16/9/14 12-10pm Beaulieu Rd.	Arrived Beaulieu Rd Stn. Informed camp at Lyndhurst. Marched forthwith.	W.O. stated articles applied for would be issued at Base in France(?)
3pm 16/9/14.	Drew part of Equipment which had arrived from Ordnance at Portsmouth. Incomplete Equipment in every branch but Divisional Ordnance rendered every assistance.	
16/9/14 to 30/9/14.	Remaining equipment gradually obtained — Personnel instructed in probable duties. Three entrainments of Sick carried out. Personnel mobilised in essentials by 26/9/14. Lectures given in afternoon to Divisional ~~Of~~ V.O.s with no previous Military Experience.	

[illegible signature]

Instructions regarding War Diaries and Intelligence Summaries are contained in F. S. Regs., Part II. and the Staff Manual respectively. Title pages will be prepared in manuscript.

WAR DIARY
or
~~INTELLIGENCE SUMMARY~~ October 1914.
(Erase heading not required.)

Army Form C. 2118.

Hour, Date, Place	Summary of Events and Information	Remarks and references to Appendices
1-30am 5/10/14	Left Lyndhurst for Southampton	
6am 5/10/14	Arrived at Docks Southampton	
4pm 5/10/14.	Embarkation on Armenian completed	
5am 7/10/14	Arrived at Zeebrugge.	
7am 7/10/14	Section ready to move –	
7pm 7/10/14	after collecting sick from transports & entraining same for Bruges – next point of halt for Division, no information re Bases or Vety Hospitals being available. Section moved in Rear of Division to Bruges by Road.	
12-30am 8/10/14	in Bruges Billetted in Cav. Bks.	
7am 8/10/14.	Left Bruges for Ostend on being informed Division was entraining at that point. Owing to orders re Section being issued by Divisional Staff – left in Rear of Division. 4 horses destroyed en route belonging to units of Division.	
6pm 8/10/14.	Found HQ 22 I.B. – they did not know where Div HQ were – marched in to Ostend – Bivouacked for night by Roadside	
9am 9/10/14	Saw ADVS – no information re Vety Bases or Hospital arrangements. Decided if Division advanced to form Temporary Stationary Hospital until information could be obtained as only means of saving many horses temporarily unfit to move. ADVS left for Bruges.	

1247 W 3299 200,000 (E) 8/14 J.B.C. & A. Forms/C. 2118/11.

Instructions regarding War Diaries and Intelligence Summaries are contained in F. S. Regs., Part II. and the Staff Manual respectively. Title pages will be prepared in manuscript.

WAR DIARY
or
~~INTELLIGENCE SUMMARY~~
(Erase heading not required.)

Oct 1914

Army Form C. 2118.

Hour, Date, Place	Summary of Events and Information	Remarks and references to Appendices
2pm. 10/10/14	Left ~~Bruges~~ Ostend for ~~Ostend~~ Bruges.	
6pm. 10/10/14	arr Bruges – Billeted in St Michel for night – received letter from ADVS. stating some sick to be collected & suitable site for Hospital at Nursery at St Andre	
7am 11/10/14.	Formed Hospital at St Andre & arranged to collect sick left behind by Division – Communicated with ADVS who had proceeded to Beernem with DHQ (Telephone)	
6pm. 11/10/14.	Having collected over 30 sick – communicated with LOC Commandant at Ostend – as situation did not appear particularly salubrious –	
7pm. 11/10/14	No 4 Section AVC. Left [illegible] arrived at St Andre bringing sick to 47 in number.	
[illegible]am 12/10/14	ADVS. 7 Div. communicated by telephone – 20 sick left at Beernem by Division – Could I collect? – DHQ moving South	
12 noon 12/10/14	Heard Ghent occupied by Germans (Telephone communication interrupted) – News from unofficial sources –	
12.15 pm. 12/10/14	Left Bruges for Beernem to obtain Horses – Took limited party only in case rapid retreat should be advisable	

Instructions regarding War Diaries and Intelligence Summaries are contained in F. S. Regs., Part II. and the Staff Manual respectively. Title pages will be prepared in manuscript.

WAR DIARY
or
~~INTELLIGENCE SUMMARY~~ October 1914

(Erase heading not required.)

Army Form C. 2118.

Hour, Date, Place	Summary of Events and Information	Remarks and references to Appendices
6pm. 12-10-14.	Entrainment of Horses at Beernem Completed — but Station master informed me impossible to send to Bruges there was no Engine available.	
5.15 p. 12/10/14.	Saw Burgomaster Beernem who informed me Germans some distance past Ghent.	
5/30pm. 12/10/14	Left Beernem for Bruges.	
7 p. 12/10/14	Arr Bruges & immediately telephoned to L of C Ostend to see whether evacuation of Sick was possible by train as on my return to Bruges, No 14 Section has left leaving all Sick. — Told to Order Train from Station master Bruges.	
2 midnight —	Entrainment of Section Horses & 51 sick completed.	
7.45am 13/10/14	Left Bruges — took four stragglers with me.	
11am — 13/10/14	Arr Thourout watered & fed	
2 p 13/10/14	Arr Dixmude. — watered & fed 4 p. — left 6 p.	
8am 14/10/14 —	Arr Dunkirk — 3 horses dead in trucks, all R.H.G.	
9am 14/10/14	Saw L of C. Staff Officer — Explained situation — left warrants for forage for horses & Rations for men etc —	

1247 W 3299 200,000 (E) 8/14 J.B.C. & A. Forms/C. 2118/11.

Instructions regarding War Diaries and Intelligence Summaries are contained in F. S. Regs., Part II. and the Staff Manual respectively. Title pages will be prepared in manuscript.

WAR DIARY
or
~~INTELLIGENCE SUMMARY~~

(Erase heading not required.)

Army Form C. 2118.

Hour, Date, Place	Summary of Events and Information	Remarks and references to Appendices
7p. 15-10-14	Horses picketted on Race Course.	
8p – 15-10-14	Horses & wagon of No 14 Section handed over to me – informed this Section proceeding to Boulogne by boat.	
8am – 15-10-15	Received orders to leave for Boulogne by Route march –	
	Four horses destroyed – before leaving –	
10am 15/10/15	Left Dunkirk with seventy one horses. – Strength 18. including officer	
6pm 15/10/15	Halted & bivouacked at farm of M. H. Bouré W of Gravelines.	
	Two horses destroyed en route –	
9am – 16/10/15	Started for Calais – left 4 horses at M. Bouré's farm – for rest & grazing	
7p – 16/10/15	Halted for night between Calais & Boulogne –	
3p. 17/10/15 –	arrived at Pont de Briques near Boulogne & Bivouacked there –	
10am 18/10/15.	Received orders from ADVS 7th Div. to rejoin as soon as possible – Handed Sick over to OC [illegible]	
8p – 18/10/15	Entrained for IV Corps Railhead	
2am – 19/10/15	Changed trains at Calais.	
8am – 19/10/15	arrived Hazebrouck.	
1p – 19/10/15	Left Hazebrouck	
2p – 19/10/15	arrived Caestre & detrained – proceeded to Poperinghe & billetted there	
7am – 20/10/15.	Left for YPRES.	
9a – 20/10/15	arrived YPRES –	
10am – 20/10/15.	Reported to ADVS.	

1247 W 3299 200,000 (E) 8/14 J.B.C. & A. Forms/C. 2118/11.

Instructions regarding War Diaries and Intelligence Summaries are contained in F. S. Regs., Part II. and the Staff Manual respectively. Title pages will be prepared in manuscript.

WAR DIARY
or
~~INTELLIGENCE SUMMARY~~
(Erase heading not required.)

Army Form C. 2118.

Hour, Date, Place	Summary of Events and Information	Remarks and references to Appendices
4 pm. 20/10/15.	Moved into Infantry Barracks.	
10/30 am 21/10/15	28 Sick & wounded entrained for Havre. Some from Cav Div.	
1 pm – 21/10/15	Moved into Cavalry ~~B~~ School – informed A D V S & left orderlies at Station & Infantry Barracks.	
10 am. 22/10/15.	24 horses 7th Div & 24 of 3rd Cav Div railed to ~~[illegible]~~ Havre	
23/10/15	8 horses 7th Div + 26 of 3rd Cav Div railed to Rouen.	
24/10/14 to 30/10/15.	Eighty horses of 7th Division and 12 of other formations sent to Hospital. All had wounds dressed – and were watered & fed immediately prior to Departure.	
31/10/14.	Eighteen horses sent to Abbeville. Billet hit by Shrapnel Shell	
	Strength of Section not big enough to deal properly with the number of Casualties & horses should be accompanied in trucks or on train by watering & Feeding parties in case they are held up en route. Railway Transport seems subject to delays –	
	J. H. Souter [illegible]	

1247 W 3299 200,000 (E) 8/14 J.B.C. & A. Forms/C. 2118/11.

Instructions regarding War Diaries and Intelligence Summaries are contained in F. S. Regs., Part II. and the Staff Manual respectively. Title pages will be prepared in manuscript.

WAR DIARY

or

~~INTELLIGENCE SUMMARY~~ November 1914.

(Erase heading not required.)

Army Form C. 2118.

Hour, Date, Place	Summary of Events and Information	Remarks and references to Appendices
1 - 11 - 14 - midnight	YPRES Shelled with H. E. Shells. Heard 17 - of which 14 exploded - First four burst near Cavalry Barracks nearest 6 yds from wall - over eighty horses in Charge.	
2 - 11 - 14.	no further Shelling 76 horses entrained - 2p. moved out to Dickebush for night	
6am. 3/11/14	Returned to YPRES. Cavalry Bks - Collected 21 horses during day. Town continuously shelled with H. E. & Shrapnel - Station hit & Railway Service Stopped.	
5p.	moved with Section & sick horses to Poperinghe.	
10-30am 4/11/14.	Rested horses to [illegible] & Returned to Cav Bks YPRES at 1p - with mounted Party. Collected at YPRES & POPERINGE - daily - railing from latter place.	
7/11/14.	Proceeded from POPERINGE to BAILLEUL on withdrawal of 7th Division from YPRES.	
18/11/14	Left for SAILLY.	
21/11/14	Changed Section to Fn Sengier. CROIX du BAC. Collected daily 8 to 10 am.	

J J McSontar [signature]

1247 W 3299 200,000 (E) 8/14 J.B.C. & A. Forms/C. 2118/11.

Instructions regarding War Diaries and Intelligence Summaries are contained in F. S. Regs., Part II. and the Staff Manual respectively. Title pages will be prepared in manuscript.

WAR DIARY

or

INTELLIGENCE SUMMARY

(Erase heading not required.)

Army Form C. 2118.

Nov. 1914.

Hour, Date, Place	Admitted	Transferred	Died or Destroyed	Reissued	Remarks and references to Appendices
YPRES 1-11-14.	17	–	–	–	
2-11-14	8	39	–	–	
POPERINGE 3-11-14	24	–	–	–	
4-11-14.	61	21	2	–	Includes 59 of 3rd Cav. Div.
5-11-14	13	–	–	–	
6-11-14.	16.	–	1	–	
7-11-14	–	88	–	–	
BAILLEUL 8-11-14	5	–	–	–	
9-11-14.	18	16.	–	–	
10-11-14	39.	34	–	–	
11-11-14.	13	16.	–	–	
12-11-14.	12.	–	–	–	
13-11-14	14	16	–	–	
14-11-14	38*	–	–	–	Includes 23 of 2nd Div.
15-11-14.	13	62*	–	–	
SAILLY 16-11-14	5	–	–	–	
17-11-14		–	–	–	
18-11-14	1	–	1	–	
CROIX du BAC 19-11-14	14	–	–	–	
20-11-14	13	–	–	–	
21-11-14	10	–	1	–	
22-11-14.	5	–	–	–	
23-11-14	1	39	–	1	
24-11-14.	10	–	1	1	
25-11-14.	16	–	1	–	
26/11/14.	4	–	–	–	
27/11/14.	20	20	–	–	
28-11-14	5	–	–	1	
29-11-14	3	–	–	–	
30-11-14	6	–	1	–	
	307.	269.	9	3.	

Instructions regarding War Diaries and Intelligence Summaries are contained in F. S. Regs., Part II. and the Staff Manual respectively. Title pages will be prepared in manuscript.

WAR DIARY
or
INTELLIGENCE SUMMARY
(Erase heading not required.)

Dec. 1914.

Army Form C. 2118.

Hour, Date, Place	Summary of Events and Information	Remarks and references to Appendices
CROIX du BAC		
8/12/15.	D.V.S. Circular Letter 738/14 re Mange received – detailing procedure to be adopted.	JJMcS
14/12/15.	D.V.S Wire – No 296 – received re telegrams to be sent when mange or suspected mange cases are sent down to Base	JJMcS
16/12/15.	D.D.V.S. Circ. Memo. No 3 received. Re Reporting cases of Injury to Sick Horses in Transit to Base.	JJMcS
16/12/15.	DDVS Wire No 404 received re Skin Cases to Abbeville others to BOULOGNE	JJMcS
	JJMcSoutar.	

1247 W 3299 200,000 (E) 8/14 J.B.C. & A. Forms/C. 2118/11.

Instructions regarding War Diaries and Intelligence Summaries are contained in F. S. Regs., Part II. and the Staff Manual respectively. Title pages will be prepared in manuscript.

WAR DIARY
or
INTELLIGENCE SUMMARY

(Erase heading not required.)

Dec 1914

Army Form C. 2118.

Hour, Date, Place	Summary of Events and Information				Remarks and references to Appendices
Croix du Bac	Admitted	Transferred	Died or Destroyed	Reissued	
1 - 12 - 14	1	–	–	–	
2 - 12 - 14	1	16	–	–	
3 - 12 - 14	8	–	–	–	
4 - 12 - 14.	–	–	–	–	
5 - 12 - 14.	–	–	1	–	
6 - 12 - 14.	2	–	2	–	
7 - 12 - 14	5	–	–	–	
8 - 12 - 14	4	–	–	1	
9 - 12 - 14	1	–	1	–	
10 - 12 - 14.	2	26	–	1	
11 - 12 - 14.	1	–	–	–	
12 - 12 - 14	–	–	–	–	
13 - 12 - 14.	4	–	–	–	
14 - 12 - 14.	5	13	–	–	
15 - 12 - 14.	6	–	1	–	
16 - 12 - 14	5	–	–	1	
17 - 12 - 14.	12	–	–	–	
18 - 12 - 14.	7	31	–	1.	
19 - 12 - 14.	6	–	1	–	
20 - 12 - 14.	2	–	–	–	
21 - 12 - 14.	5	–	1	–	
22 - 12 - 14.	4	–	–	–	
23 - 12 - 14	8	–	–	–	
24 - 12 - 14.	–	–	–	2	
25 - 12 - 14.	4	–	1	1	
26 - 12 - 14.	1	15	–	1	
27 - 12 - 14	2	–	–	–	
28 - 12 - 14.	2	–	–	–	
29 - 12 - 14.	–	–	1	–	
30 - 12 - 14.	5	–	–	3	
31 - 12 - 14.	5	–	–	–	
Totals	108.	101.	9 –	11.	

7th Division

121
4586

No 12. Mobile Vety: Section.

Vol I.

~~Feb 1915~~

1 Jan - 28 Feb 1915

Instructions regarding War Diaries and Intelligence Summaries are contained in F. S. Regs., Part II. and the Staff Manual respectively. Title pages will be prepared in manuscript.

WAR DIARY

or

~~INTELLIGENCE SUMMARY~~

(Erase heading not required.)

Jan. 1915.

Army Form C. 2118.

Hour, Date, Place	Summary of Events and Information	Remarks and references to Appendices
Croix du Bac.		
11-1-15.	Extract from D.V.S letter No 74/15 received. Re. Ashes or Substitutes in trucks, & old & useless horses being sent down.	Both points had been attended to previous to receipt of letter. [illegible]
20-1-15.	Wire No 32. from D.D.V.S "Mange cases to be sent to Hesdigneul.	[illegible]
21-1-15.	Five suspected Mange cases sent to Hesdigneul.	[illegible]
23-1-15.	Conducting party reports mange cases were sent to Abbeville by Railway Authorities.	[illegible]
24-1-15.	Saw R.T.O. at Steenwerck & he informs me his instructions are to send all suspected mange & mange cases to Abbeville.	[illegible]
31-1-15.	In view of sending suspected mange cases away tomorrow. Saw R.T.O again. He informs me his orders are still to send such cases to Abbeville.	[illegible]

[illegible signature]

1247 W 3299 200,000 (E) 8/14 J.B.C. & A. Forms/C. 2118/11.

WAR DIARY
or
~~INTELLIGENCE~~ SUMMARY
(Erase heading not required.)

Army Form C. 2118.

Instructions regarding War Diaries and Intelligence Summaries are contained in F. S. Regs., Part II. and the Staff Manual respectively. Title pages will be prepared in manuscript.

Jan 1915

Hour, Date, Place	Summary of Events and Information				Remarks and references to Appendices
Croix du Bac.	Admitted.	Transferred.	Destroyed or Died.	Reissued.	
1-1-15.	3	16	–	–	
2-~~8~~1-15.	3	–	–	1	
3-1-15.	8	–	1	–	
4-1-15.	8	–	2	–	
5-1-15.	4	–	2	–	
6-1-15	1	–	–	1.	
7-1-15.	2	–	–	4.	
8-1-15.	1	24	1	–	
9-1-15	3	–	–	–	
10-1-15.	6	–	–	–	
11-1-15.	2	–	–	–	
12-1-15.	1	–	–	–	
13-1-15.	–	–	–	–	
14-1-15.	2	3	–	–	
15-1-15.	1	–	6	1	
16-1-15.	9	–	–	–	
17-1-15	17	–	–	–	
18-1-15.	2	24	–	1.	
19-1-15.	7	–	–	–	
20-1-15.	11	–	3	–	
21-1-15.	1	25.	–	–	
22-1-15	7	–	–	–	
23-1-15.	3	–	–	1	
24-1-15.	1	–	–	–	
25-1-15	5	–	–	–	
26-1-15.	12	–	2	1	
27-1-15	2	21	–	4.	
28-1-15.	4	–	–	–	
29-1-15	5	–	–	–	
30-1-15.	12	–	–	–	
31-1-15.	3.	39	–	–	
Totals	146	152.	17	14.	

[illegible]

Instructions regarding War Diaries and Intelligence Summaries are contained in F. S. Regs., Part II. and the Staff Manual respectively. Title pages will be prepared in manuscript.

WAR DIARY
or
INTELLIGENCE SUMMARY
(Erase heading not required.)

Feb. 1915

Army Form C. 2118.

N° 12 MOBILE VETERINARY SECTION 12 MAR. 1915 11/15

Hour, Date, Place	Summary of Events and Information	Remarks and references to Appendices
4/2/15. Croix du Bac.	D.V.S. Circ memo. No. 12. dated 31/1/15. received. re. Skin Disease - Dressings + Diagnosis.	JJMcL
8/2/15. " "	D.V.S. Circ memo. No. 13 dated 4/2/15 received re. states + returns.	JJMcL
13/2/15 " "	D.D.V.S. Correspondence re ineffective horses to be sent to No 3. Advanced Remount Depot Boulogne. - received also includes mares in foal.	JJMcL.
		A pair Stewart's Clippers received but no spare plates. The lack of a float is still a great handicap especially in dealing with foot cases.
	J.J. McSoutar	J.J. McSoutar

Instructions regarding War Diaries and Intelligence Summaries are contained in F. S. Regs., Part II. and the Staff Manual respectively. Title pages will be prepared in manuscript.

WAR DIARY
or
~~INTELLIGENCE~~ SUMMARY
(Erase heading not required.)

Feb. 1915

Army Form C. 2118.

Hour, Date, Place	Admitted	Transferred to Hospital	Destroyed	Reissued	Remarks and references to Appendices
Croix du Bac.					
1/2/15.	5.	14.	–	2	
2/2/15.	nil	nil.	nil	1.	
3/2/15.	1	nil	nil	nil	On Course.
4/2/15.	1	nil.	1	2.	
5/2/15.	1	nil	nil	–	
6/2/15.	2.	–	–	–	
7/2/15.	1	–	–	–	
8/2/15	2	–	–	–	
9/2/15.	2	–	–	–	
10/2/15	3	–	–	–	
11/2/15.	11	–	1	–	
12/2/15	2	–	–	–	
13/2/15	7	19	–	–	
14/2/15.	4	–	–	–	
15/2/15.	12	–	–	1.	Instructed to send mares to No 3 Remt Depot also Cast horses to Vet Hosp.
16/2/15	3	–	3	–	
17/2/15.	6	–	–	–	
18/2/15	6.	19.	–	–	3 mares in foal.
19/2/15.	7	–	–	–	
20/2/15.	5	–	–	1	
21/2/15.	7	16	–	–	
22/2/15	1	–	–	1	
23/2/15.	4	–	–	–	
24/2/15	3	–	–	–	
25/2/15	5	–	–	–	
26/2/15	3	15	2	–	
27/2/15.	2 3.	–	1	8	
28/2/15.	4	16	–	6	

Totals: Adm. 130. Trans 99 Died or Destr. 8 Remounts 22.

[illegible signature]

7th Division

12th Mobile Vety: Section

Vol II 4 — 31. 3. 15.

Instructions regarding War Diaries and Intelligence Summaries are contained in F. S. Regs., Part II. and the Staff Manual respectively. Title pages will be prepared in manuscript.

WAR DIARY
or
~~INTELLIGENCE SUMMARY~~
(Erase heading not required.)

March 1915 — 12 MVS

Army Form C. 2118.

Hour, Date, Place	Summary of Events and Information	Remarks and references to Appendices
4 pm. 4-3-15. Croix du Bac	Left Fm Sergier for Bleulow. Vieux Berquin. Two horses handed over to No 6 Section. JJMcL	These could have been entrained had float been available JJMcL
6 pm. 4-3-15 Bleulow	arrived at Fm Traulles - or near Fm Hullebert JJMcL	
8 am 8-3-15 "	Advance party sent to Estaires to prepare billets. JJMcL	
3.30 pm 8-3-15. "	Section left for Estaires. Cattle Killer indented for 23-10-14. received. JJMcL	Seemingly unnecessary delay
5.30 pm. 8-3-15 ESTAIRES	Section arrived ESTAIRES. billetted in Timber Yard. JJMcL	
5. pm 9-3-15 ESTAIRES	Verbal notification from ADMS, 7th Division that No. 835 Pte C.H. Lester is suspected of suffering from Cerebro Spinal Meningitis - Daily inspection by M.O. JJMcL	
14-3-15 ESTAIRES.	Copy of Telegram re Glanders in La Bassée received. JJMcL Coloured labels for sick received. They are too small and writing in indelible pencil makes little impression + washes off all except the white labels easily.	
23-3-15. ESTAIRES	Notification received from O.C. No 10 Stationary Hospital of Pte Lester's death there on 20-3-15. Orders received from DAQMG that Section is to be clear of Estaires by 3 pm on 25th inst. Billets allotted in any farm unoccupied in Squares K31 + L31 - Some of these farms visited none found unoccupied. Made arrangements to send off sick from La Gorgue Station instead of MERVILLE. JJMcL	
26-3-15. ESTAIRES.	Left ESTAIRES. for Farm near MERVILLE Station.	
27-3-15	Left Farm and entered billets previously occupied by No 15 M.V.S just W of MERVILLE on road to BASSE BOULOGNE.	

1247 W 3299 200,000 (E) 8/14 J.B.C. & A. Forms/C. 2118/11.

Instructions regarding War Diaries and Intelligence Summaries are contained in F. S. Regs., Part II. and the Staff Manual respectively. Title pages will be prepared in manuscript.

WAR DIARY
or
~~INTELLIGENCE SUMMARY~~
(Erase heading not required.)

March 1915. 12th M.V.S.

Hour, Date, Place	Summary of Events and Information	Remarks and references to Appendices
29-3-15. MERVILLE	Rations drawn twice in one day. In afternoon direct from Railhead – in other words two days Rations are in hand and have to be carried on a move which if a move has to be made involves a strain on available Transport.	
31-3-15. MERVILLE.	Section still at MERVILLE. During the past month it has become more evident how greatly the mobility of a Section is hindered by not having any means of disposing of animals which are temporarily unable to walk. While the Section remains in one place, such cases can be treated for a week or even longer and be so far improved as to be able to walk to ~~the~~ a Station for sending to Hospital. When however several of such cases are on hand and a move takes place, unless a Station is very close to the Section they cannot be disposed of in this way, with the present Equipment of a M.V.S. Speaking generally these cases are those which require constant Veterinary attention, especially in their earlier Stages, and if left behind without this they will probably be useless when an opportunity to collect them occurs. The only alternative is to destroy them, and this seems unnecessarily wasteful and in my opinion does not reflect credit upon our Divisional Departmental Organisation. The situation described above need not occur at all if a light Horse Float was in possession of the M.V. Section. Such cases could then be collected at once ~~and~~ attended to, and sent to the Base Hospitals immediately. When the Section is moving from one point to another	

1247 W 3299 200,000 (E) 8/14 J.B.C. & A. Forms/C. 2118/11.

Instructions regarding War Diaries and Intelligence Summaries are contained in F. S. Regs., Part II. and the Staff Manual respectively. Title pages will be prepared in manuscript.

WAR DIARY
or
~~INTELLIGENCE SUMMARY~~
(Erase heading not required.)

March 1915

Army Form C. 2118.

12th MVS

Hour, Date, Place	Summary of Events and Information	Remarks and references to Appendices
31-3-15 (Contd.)	the float could be used to carry forage and would be infinitely more useful for this purpose than the G.S. Forage Cart at present part of the Section Equipment. * J J McSoutar [?] Capt AVC * It is possible that the above considerations do not apply with equal force to the M.V.S. with Cavalry Brigades but the experience, of the past four months, especially has forced the conclusion upon me that a float would be of immeasurable benefit to a MVS with an Infantry Division. JJM	

1247 W 3299 200,000 (E) 8/14 J.B.C. & A. Forms/C. 2118/11.

Army Form C. 2118.

Instructions regarding War Diaries and Intelligence Summaries are contained in F. S. Regs., Part II. and the Staff Manual respectively. Title pages will be prepared in manuscript.

WAR DIARY
or
~~INTELLIGENCE SUMMARY~~

(*Erase heading not required.*)

March 1915. 12 M.V.S.

Hour, Date, Place	Summary of Events and Information				Remarks and references to Appendices
Croix du Bac. 1-3-15.	Admitted.	Transferred to V.H.	Destroyed.	Reissued.	
1-3-15.	7.	-	-	-	
2-3-15	3	-	-	-	
3-3-15	-	-	-	-	
Blaton Vieux Berquin 4-3-15	-	8	-	2*	*Passed to No 6 M.V.S. [illegible] (Lt. [illegible])
5-3-15	-	-	-	-	
6-3-15.	1	-	-	-	
7-3-15	2	-	-	-	
ESTAIRES. 8-3-15	-	-	-	-	
9-3-15.	32	-	-	15	
10-3-15	2	-	-	7.	
11-3-15	6	8	-	-	
12-3-15	11	19.	-	-	
13-3-15.	5	-	1	1	
14-3-15.	4	-	-	1.	
15-3-15.	3.	8.	1	-	
16-3-15.	12.	-	1	1	
17-3-15	10.	11	-	1	
18-3-15	5	-	-	1	
19-3-15	4	8	-	-	
20-3-15	2	-	-	1	
21-3-15.	10	8	-	1	
22-3-15	16.	8	-	1	
23-3-15.	7	-	-	4	
24-3-15	7	28	-	4.	
25-3-15	5	-	-	1	
MERVILLE 26-3-15	8	-	-	-	
27-3-15	3	-	-	-	
28-3-15.	4	8	-	-	
29-3-15	9	-	-	-	
30-3-15	4	15	1	-	
31-3-15	14	-	-	1	
	195	129	4	42.	

1247 W 3299 200,000 (E) 8/14 J.B.C. & A. Forms/C. 2118/11.

121/5268

7th Division

No 12. Mobile Vety Section

Vol III 1 – 29. 4. 15.

Ms.

Instructions regarding War Diaries and Intelligence Summaries are contained in F. S. Regs., Part II. and the Staff Manual respectively. Title pages will be prepared in manuscript.

WAR DIARY
or
~~INTELLIGENCE SUMMARY~~
(Erase heading not required.)

April. 1915.

Army Form C. 2118.

Hour, Date, Place	Summary of Events and Information	Remarks and references to Appendices
MERVILLE.		
1-4-15.	Received letter DDVS 1st Army No 74/29/3/15 V.S. re Mobile Sections not being overburdened with Veterinary Equipment	
7-4-15.	Letter from DDVS – ADVS V 179/15. recd. re [illegible] number of horses Evacuated by Section.	
16-4-15	Recd Copy of Letter from French Mission No 1066 D.E.S. dated 7/4/15 re existence of Infectious disease – Northern provinces of France.	
17-4-15	Section inspected by the D.V.S.	
17-4-15.	Recd letter re entrainment of Sick horses – attaching to Supply Trains instead of to French Commercial Trains. Latter procedure causing great delay in arrival of Horses.	undoubtedly so but Station masters are experts at their own work + one finds that Supply trains are sometimes so heavy when empty that they cannot tackle the gradients with the Engines at disposal.
18-4-15.	Recd letter D.V.S. /14/1034/15. Re 'Cast' Remount Cases.	
28-4-15	Division minus certain troops, moved north. Received notification of 5 horses being left behind – alleged unable to move.	
29-4-15.	Took mounted party + visited horses left behind. two Shot – two entrained direct and one (Pneumonia Case) left with Farmer M. Edouard Ridez. Rue de la Bassée just South of Railway.	VOs leave horses behind which should have been shot days before. fear divisional order re referring to ADVS prior to Destruction during [illegible].
	Note Once more I must record the difficulty of dealing with a percentage of sick horses without a float. the loss of horses in the division as a direct cause of there being no float with a Mobile Section, must reach almost 30 a month.	
	J. J. McSomber	

1247 W 3299 200,000 (E) 8/14 J.B.C. & A. Forms/C. 2118/11.

Instructions regarding War Diaries and Intelligence Summaries are contained in F. S. Regs., Part II. and the Staff Manual respectively. Title pages will be prepared in manuscript.

WAR DIARY
or
~~INTELLIGENCE SUMMARY~~
(Erase heading not required.)

Army Form C. 2118.

April 1915. 12th M.V.S.

Hour, Date, Place	Summary of Events and Information				Remarks and references to Appendices
	Admitted	Transferred	Died or Destroyed	Returned to units	
MERVILLE 1-4-15.	6.	–	–	–	
2-4-15.	22	30.	1	–	
3-4-15	4	8.	–	–	
4-4-15.	3	–	–	–	
5-4-15	–	–	–	–	
6-4-15	3	–	1	–	
7-4-15.	4	8	–	–	
8-4-15.	7	–	1	–	
9-4-15.	5	16.	–	–	
10-4-15.	4	–	2	2	
11-4-15	3	–	–	–	
12-4-15.	11	8	–	–	
13-4-15.	5	–	–	–	
14-4-15	6	16	–	–	
15-4-15	–	–	–	–	
16-4-15	4	–	–	–	
17-4-15	4	–	–	–	
18-4-15.	1	8	–	–	
19-4-15.	18.*	–	–	–	* Includes 5 Cast by Remounts.
20-4-15.	7	28	–	– *	
21-4-15.	3	–	–	–	
22-4-15.	4	–	–	–	
23-4-15	–	–	–	–	
24-4-15	4	8×	–	–	× Includes 1 to R. Division.
25-4-15.	7	–	–	–	
26-4-15	3	–	1	–	
27-4-15	1 ①	8.	–	–	① Mare in foal
28-4-15.	5	–	2	–	
29-4-15		15.	–	1	
30-4-15.	5.	–	–	–	
		153.	8.	3.	J. McCarter

7th Division

171/5576

No 12 Mobile Vety. Section.

Vol IV 1 — 31.5.15

R.W.

Instructions regarding War Diaries and Intelligence Summaries are contained in F. S. Regs., Part II. and the Staff Manual respectively. Title pages will be prepared in manuscript.

WAR DIARY
or
~~INTELLIGENCE SUMMARY~~
(Erase heading not required.)

May 1915.

Army Form C. 2118.

Hour, Date, Place	Summary of Events and Information	Remarks and references to Appendices
1 - 5 - 15	~~Recd. Horse Artillery unit left behind in October 1914. Sarcoptic mange.~~	
2 - 5 - 15. 7.30 p.m.	Received orders to move to PRADELLES on 3-5-15.	
3 - 5 - 15. 3 p.	Moved off from MERVILLE for PRADELLES leaving a collecting party behind. Sick Horses admitted 1-5-15.	
6 p.	Arrived PRADELLES	
7 pm.	Received note asking for float to collect two Sick Horses unable to move. - 27th Bde R.G.A.	
4 - 5 - 15. 6.30 am.	Proceeded to inspect two horses left behind at Nord Helf.	
11 am.	Left PRADELLES. Transport sent ahead to MERVILLE. Two mounted men left behind to collect at PRADELLES - with orders to leave there at 4 pm. Proceeded with mounted Party to ~~PRADELLES~~ NORD HELF and then MERRIS. At MERRIS found two horses Queens Regiment unable to move. Butcher at MERRIS had float but it was in use. Proceeded to BLEUTOUR and attempted to hire float there. Float was away. Returned to MERVILLE	
5 - 5 - 15. 6 a.	Sent party under Staff Sgt Haydon to pick up float + collect the two horses at NORD HELF. Party returned at 10 am - float not available.	
6 p.	Received intimation of Horse of 7 D A C. left behind at VIEUX BERQUIN. Foot Case.	
6 - 5 - 15.	Took Shoeing Smith + proceeded to case at VIEUX BERQUIN. Dressed it. Float available. Sent out party - collected one horse from NORD HELF Other case kick inside Tibia had led to fracture - so was destroyed.	
7 - 5 - 15	Collected two horses from MERRIS - one from VIEUX BERQUIN.	

W 3299 200,000 (E) 8/14 J.B.C. & A. Forms/C. 2118/11.

Instructions regarding War Diaries and Intelligence Summaries are contained in F. S. Regs., Part II. and the Staff Manual respectively. Title pages will be prepared in manuscript.

WAR DIARY
or
~~INTELLIGENCE SUMMARY~~
(Erase heading not required.)

May. 1915.

Army Form C. 2118.

12 M.V.S.

Hour, Date, Place	Summary of Events and Information	Remarks and references to Appendices
7-5-15. 7pm	Received orders to move to ESTAIRES. Sgt Butler joined from No 10 V.H.	
8-5-15.	Moved to ESTAIRES, loading horses 'en route'. Staff Sgt Hagydon & L/Cpl Louden sent to No 7 V.H. RTO at La GORGUE informed me these horses were to be sent to ABBEVILLE in accordance with his instructions. I have not received any intimation of this from the Veterinary Authorities and my orders are at present to send all horses to Neufchatel Hospital.	Notified DDVS on usual Wire.
9-5-15	A further consignment of horses sent off - also sent to ABBEVILLE by RTO.	
11-5-15.	Third consignment of horses sent off - also to ABBEVILLE. Still no instructions received. Conducting party sent on 8/5/15 returns & Corporal Kerby reports horses unloaded 9/5/15. Delay in return due to his proceeding to Neufchatel Pdc for Stores. Shoeing Smith Adams transferred to No 8 M.V.S direct.	
12-5-15	Conducting party of 9/5/15 returned & Pte Knowles i/charge reports horses arrived at ABBEVILLE at 4.15pm. 10/5/15. but were not unloaded until 2pm on 11/5/15. No forage could be obtained at ABBEVILLE & horses were consequently left without forage all morning of 11th as forage sent only for 9th & 10th.	
14-5-15	Conducting party sent on 11th returned & reports horses not unloaded until noon on 13th although they arrived there evening (a.p.) of 12th)	
15-5-15.	Horses sent away. Advance party sent on to Le Hamel to Collect Sick.	

W 3299 200,000 (E) 8/14 J.B.C. & A. Forms/C. 2118/11.

Instructions regarding War Diaries and Intelligence Summaries are contained in F. S. Regs., Part II. and the Staff Manual respectively. Title pages will be prepared in manuscript.

WAR DIARY
or
~~INTELLIGENCE SUMMARY~~
(Erase heading not required.)

Army Form C. 2118.

May 1915 — 12th Mobile Vet^y Section.

Hour, Date, Place	Summary of Events and Information	Remarks and references to Appendices
ESTAIRES 16-5-15, 930am.	Section moved off to BETHUNE. Billeted in field near Station Town	
	Shelled during night. 12.25 – 3.20am	
BETHUNE 18-5-15.	Horses sent off – as 4 had been admitted belonging to London Division	
	these were sent + O.C. London Div M.V.S. sent four – to go with them	
20-5-15.	Proceeded to MERVILLE – saw mare left behind there – left her	
	with farmer. M Roussell near the Sort. Returned to BETHUNE	
	No SR 19 Sgt. H. Drury wounded by Shell fire. (slightly = leg)	
21-5-15. 10am.	Section moved to Lillers	
LILLERS 23-5-15	made arrangements with RTO for consignments – as necessary	
24-5-15	Received orders to report to W.O. on being relieved by [redacted]	
	Capt P.D. Carey.	
27-5-15	Capt P.D. Carey AVC arrived to take over Section.	J.J.McSoutar Capt AVC.
27.5.15.	Arrived LILLERS reported arrival to R.T.O. & to A.D.V.S. Took over duties of O.C. No 12 Mobile Vet Section from Capt Soutar	
28.5.15	Sent off 13 horses to No 5 Hospital.	
29.5.15	Went to MERVILLE to see mare that had been left behind. Found that she died on the 28.5.15. Was informed by Mr Roussell that he reported the death to some officer who saw the mare dead & who told him that he would inform me. No information yet received	
30.5.15	Conducting party returned. Although the horses were boxed at 3p.m on Friday they arrived ABBEVILLE 5.30pm on Saturday & were not disentrained until 9.30 the following morning.	

P. D. Carey
Capt AVC

W 3299 200,000 (E) 8/14 J.B.C. & A. Forms/C.2118/11.

Instructions regarding War Diaries and Intelligence Summaries are contained in F. S. Regs., Part II. and the Staff Manual respectively. Title pages will be prepared in manuscript.

WAR DIARY
or
~~INTELLIGENCE SUMMARY~~
(Erase heading not required.)

May 1915 — 12 W V S

Army Form C. 2118.

Hour, Date, Place	Summary of Events and Information				Remarks and references to Appendices
	Adm	Transf	Died or Destr	Reissued	
1-5-15.	4	-	-	-	
2-5-15.	3	12	-	-	
3-5-15.	4	-	-	-	
4-5-15.	4	-	-	-	
5-5-15.	-	7	-	-	
6-5-15.	3	-	-	-	
7-5-15.	15	-	-	-	
8-5-15	1	15	-	-	
9-5-15.	17	15	-	-	
10-5-15	16	-	-	-	
11-5-15.	-	16	-	-	
12-5-15	2	-	3	-	
13-5-15	-	-	-	-	
14-5-15	3	-	-	-	
15-5-15.	5	8	-	-	
16-5-15.	2	-	-	-	
17-5-15	10	-	-	1	
18-5-15.	8	12	-	1	
19-5-15.	3	-	-	1	
20-5-15.	2	11	-	-	
21-5-15	-	-	-	-	
22-5-15.	2	-	-	-	
23-5-15	-	-	-	-	
24-5-15	8	-	-	-	
25-5-15	7	16	-	-	
26-5-15	7	-	-	2	
27-5-15	3	13	-	-	
28-5-15	1	-	1	-	
29-5-15	1	-	-	-	
30-5-15	12.	-	-	-	
31-5-15	3	-	-	-	
Total	146	125	4	5	

7th Division

121/5870

No 12. Mobile Vety: Section

Vol V 1 – 30.6.15.

Instructions regarding War Diaries and Intelligence Summaries are contained in F. S. Regs., Part II. and the Staff Manual respectively. Title pages will be prepared in manuscript.

WAR DIARY
or
~~INTELLIGENCE SUMMARY~~
(Erase heading not required.)

Army Form C. 2118.

12th Mobile Veterinary Section

June 1915

Hour, Date, Place		Summary of Events and Information	Remarks and references to Appendices
LILLERS.	1.6.15.	Sent Conducting Party with 15 sick to ABBEVILLE & one in foal mare to BOULOGNE.	
	3.6.15	Conducting Party returned, bringing Vet' Stores. Received orders to proceed tomorrow with section to 36 Boulevard Frederick De George. BETHUNE	
BETHUNE	4.6.15	arrived BETHUNE. The Section billeted as ordered. Town shelled in afternoon.	
"	5.6.15	Inspected G.O.C's escort horses at CHOCQUES. also detachment of 18 Hussars	
		Sent 14 horses to hospital. one section horse grazed by a splinter from a bursting shell	Includes 1 mange case from 7th Div A C.
	8-6-15	Reported to A.D.V.S. that Sergt Buller [illegible] was most unsatisfactory, especially as the Senior N.C.O. of the section, & requested his removal.	
	11.6.15	Received orders that all units should be in possession of Respirators.	
	13.6.15	Respirators received & issued to the men with instructions for use.	
		Received telegram ordering Sergt Buller to proceed No 5. V.H. ABBEVILLE	
		30072. Dr Broom. W.S. from A.S.C. reported for Duty with the Section. authority for move. D.A.G. Z. 668. d/ 10-6-15. Reported his arrival to A.D.V.S.	
	14-6-15	Reported in writing to A.D.V.S. the filthy condition in which all horses from the 7th Divisional Ammunition Column are received.	
		Sergt Buller proceeded to No 5. Veterinary Hospital. ABBEVILLE.	
		Address from which a Horse Float can be obtained. Ve Lebrun-Fournier. 139. Rue de Lille. Bethune.	
		S.E. 2696 Sergt W. H. Chapman reported for Duty. Came from No 10 M.V.S.	
	15.6.15.	Took over Vet' Charge of Detachments 1st Army Signal Coy. at CHOCQUES. arranged to inspect all horses at 7 a.m. on Wednesdays & Saturdays that are stabled in CHOCQUES including officers chargers.	
	18.6.15	Received a wire from H.Qrs 20 Inf: Bde to send a Float for an injured horse, no float available today.	

Instructions regarding War Diaries and Intelligence Summaries are contained in F. S. Regs., Part II. and the Staff Manual respectively. Title pages will be prepared in manuscript.

WAR DIARY
or
INTELLIGENCE SUMMARY

(*Erase heading not required.*) 12 Mobile Veterinary Section. June 1915.

Army Form C. 2118.

Hour, Date, Place	Summary of Events and Information	Remarks and references to Appendices
BETHUNE. 18.6.15	Sergt. Spilsted. Ptes. Gallagher. Pulford. Roe. Evans. joined for duty with this section from No 3. Veterinary Hospital.	
19.6.15	Float commandeered by the French cannot get one until tomorrow. The 4 men joined with practically no kit & no rifles. They have never been issued to them.	
26.6.15.	Town shelled in the morning. As the second shell burst on a house not more than 100 yds away from the stable, sent all the sections horses out.	
30-6-15	Went to collect a horse of 118 Bde R.F.A. Found he had a fractured Pastern so shot him. Collected another horse of same Bde. Shot him also.	

P. D. Carey. Capt. A.V.C

1247 W 3299 200,000 (E) 8/14 J.B.C. & A. Forms/C. 2118/11.

Instructions regarding War Diaries and Intelligence Summaries are contained in F. S. Regs., Part II. and the Staff Manual respectively. Title pages will be prepared in manuscript.

WAR DIARY
or
INTELLIGENCE SUMMARY
(Erase heading not required.)

Army Form C. 2118.

12th Mobile Section.
JUNE 1915

Hour, Date, Place		Adm.	Transf.	Died or Destroyed.	Reissued	Remarks and references to Appendices
LILLERS.	1-6-15.	2	15	–	–	Includes 1 Infoal mare sent to Remts. open Joint.
"	2-6-15	3	–	–	–	
	3-6-15	–	–	1	1	
BETHUNE	4-6-15	5	–	–	–	
	5-6-15	6	14	–	–	
"	6-6-15	5	–	–	–	
	7-6-15	~~4~~	8	–	–	
	8-6-15	6	–	–	–	
	9-6-15	3	15	–	2	
	10-6-15	4	–	–	1	
	11-6-15	7	–	–	–	
	12-6-15	3	–	–	2.	
	13-6-15	5	16	–	–	Includes 2 mares in foal.
	14-6-15	8	–	1	–	
	15-6-15	2	–	–	–	
	16-6-15	–	16	–	–	
	17-6-15	1	–	–	–	
	18-6-15	2	–	–	–	
	19-6-15	7	–	–	–	
	20-6-15	10	–	–	1	
	21-6-15	3	16	–	–	Includes 1 mare in foal.
	22-6-15	2	–	–	–	
	23-6-15	9	–	–	–	
	24-6-15	4	14	–	1	
	26-6-15	1	–	–	–	
	27-6-15	4	–	–	–	
	28-6-15	9	–	–	–	
	29-6-15	6	18	–	1	
	30-6-15	19	–	1	–	
TOTAL.		150	132	3	9	

P. D. Carey,
Capt A.V.C.

1247 W 3299 200,000 (E) 8/14 J.B.C. & A. Forms/C. 2118/11.

7th Division

121/6206

No 12 Mobile Vety: Section

Vol VI

Instructions regarding War Diaries and Intelligence Summaries are contained in F. S. Regs., Part II. and the Staff Manual respectively. Title pages will be prepared in manuscript.

WAR DIARY
or
INTELLIGENCE SUMMARY

(Erase heading not required.) 12th Mobile Vet. Section July 1915.

Army Form C. 2118.

Hour, Date, Place		Summary of Events and Information	Remarks and references to Appendices
BETHUNE	4-7-15.	Received orders to bring the section into LILLERS tomorrow.	
LILLERS.	5-7-15	arrived Lillers with section. Camped in the same field as last time. Looked round for a better place.	
	6-7-15.	Brought the section to 6½ Rue National. Office at 51 Rue National.	
"	9-7-15	Sergt Chapman proceeded on leave to England	
"	10-7-15	Received a note from A.D.V.S. saying he was proceeding to England, detailing me to carry on his duties	
"	12-7-15	Left a mare suffering from Concussion at the farm of M. Debouchire. BUSNES.	
"	15-7-15	Collected a horse of 7th Div Train left at farm of M. Cruffed MAZINGHEM. Inspected horses of R.A.M.C.	
"	16-7-15	Interviewed the C.R.A. 7th Div. re a case of mange found in the 37th Bde. R.F.A.	
"	17-7-15	Sergt Chapman returned from leave, accompanied the C.R.A. in his inspection of 37 Bde.	
	19-7-15	Capt Harley proceeded on leave to England. Collected a horse belonging to the 2/1st South Midland Field Coy R.E. at RAIMBERT.	
	20-7-15	Collected a horse of 7 Sig Coy at BUSNES – also one of the 1st South Midland Bde at BELLINR.	
	21-7-15	Sergt Spitstead transferred to No 7 Vet Hospital. (Local Corporal No 22)	
	24-7-15	Major Glasse returned from leave, handed over duties of A.D.V.S. to him.	
	27-7-15	Collected a horse at GONNEHEM.	
	29-7-15	Collected a horse at LIERES + FERFAY.	

P. D. Carey. Capt. A.V.C.

1247 W 3299 200,000 (E) 8/14 J.B.C. & A. Forms/C. 2118/11.

Instructions regarding War Diaries and Intelligence Summaries are contained in F. S. Regs., Part II. and the Staff Manual respectively. Title pages will be prepared in manuscript.

WAR DIARY
or
INTELLIGENCE SUMMARY

(Erase heading not required.)

Army Form C. 2118.

12 Mobile Vet^y Section. July 1915

Hour, Date, Place		Adm:	Transf.	Died or Destroyed.	Received.	Remarks and references to Appendices
BETHUNE.	1 - 7 - 15.	3	19.	2.	3.	Includes 1 mare in foal.
	2 - 7 - 15	3	-	-	-	
LILLERS.	3 - 7 - 15	1	-	-	1	
	6 - 7 - 15	2	-	-	-	
	7 - 7 - 15	8	-	-	-	
	8 - 7 - 15	2	-	-	-	
	9 - 7 - 15	2	8	-	1	
	10 - 7 - 15	7	-	-	-	
	11 - 7 - 15	5	-	-	-	
	12 - 7 - 15	13	16	-	2	
	13 - 7 - 15	5	-	-	-	
	14 - 7 - 15	5	-	-	-	
	15 - 7 - 15	1	16	-	-	
	16 - 7 - 15	5	-	-	-	
	17 - 7 - 15	4	-	1	-	
	18 - 7 - 15	8	-	-	1	
	19 - 7 - 15	9	16	-	-	
	20 - 7 - 15	6	-	1	-	
	21 - 7 - 15	13	-	-	1	
	22 - 7 - 15	3	16	-	1	
	23 - 7 - 15	3	-	-	-	
	24 - 7 - 15	4	-	-	-	
	26 - 7 - 15	3	-	-	3	
	27 - 7 - 15	4	13	-	2	
	28 - 7 - 15	4	-	-	-	
	29 - 7 - 15	6	-	-	-	
	30 - 7 - 15	3	18	-	4	
	31 - 7 - 15	5	-	-	-	
				1	-	
Totals		137	122	5	25	

R. D. Carey. Capt. A.V.C.

7th Division

121/6737

No 12 Mobile Vety Section

Vol VIII

August 15

AWS

Instructions regarding War Diaries and Intelligence Summaries are contained in F. S. Regs., Part II. and the Staff Manual respectively. Title pages will be prepared in manuscript.

WAR DIARY
or
INTELLIGENCE SUMMARY
(Erase heading not required.)

Army Form C. 2118.

12th Mobile Vet. Section VII Division

Hour, Date, Place		Summary of Events and Information	Remarks and references to Appendices
LILLERS	3-8-15	Collected a horse left by XIX Div. at BOURECQ.	
"	6-8-15	Received the new "Receipt Notes" to be given to inhabitants when collecting horses.	
"	9-8-15	Sergt Chapman severely reprimanded for being in an estaminet during prohibited hours. Pte Stevens awarded 10 days C.B.	
	8-8-15	Pte Edwards admitted & transferred to hospital.	
"	12-8-15	Went with A.D.V.S. to find a suitable place for the section at LOCON.	
"	15-8-15	Orders received to proceed with section to PACAUT on the 17th. Went out there & found a suitable place for the section.	
PACAUT	17-8-15	Brought the section to PACAUT.	
"	18-8-15	This is a very bad place for a Mobile Section. The only water available both for men & horses is from a very slowly flowing stream at the side of the road, which I have learnt is not considered by the Medical Authorities to be pure. As we have no water carts we shall have to move. At some time or other a horse has evidently been buried in the field & not covered sufficiently, consequently the smell is very bad.	
"	19-8-15	Reported to the A.D.V.S. the insanitary place the section is in. Arranged with him to have a collecting station at LOCON & the section to be in Bethune. At PACAUT we are far too distant from the units to be of use. By having a collecting station at LOCON & the section at BETHUNE we are very convenient for every brigade. Two men sick today. This is no doubt due to the unhealthy place as they are both going at the lungs.	
	20-8-15	Brought the section into BETHUNE, 36 Boulevard Frederick De Georges.	
	21-8-15	Party left behind at PACAUT arrived.	
	22-8-15	Collected 2 horses left by IX Div. near Locon.	
	28-8-15	D.D.V.S. 1st Army inspected the section. No 496 Pte Sparry arrived for duty with the section.	
	31-8-15	Brought in the collecting party at LOCON to BETHUNE.	P. D. Carey. Capt. AVC

1247 W 3299 200,000 (E) 8/14 J.B.C. & A. Forms/C. 2118/11.

Instructions regarding War Diaries and Intelligence Summaries are contained in F. S. Regs., Part II. and the Staff Manual respectively. Title pages will be prepared in manuscript.

WAR DIARY
or
INTELLIGENCE SUMMARY

(Erase heading not required.)

Army Form C. 2118.

12th Mobile Vet. Section, VII Division

Hour, Date, Place		Summary of Events and Information: Adm.	Transf.	Died or destroyed	Missing	Remarks and references to Appendices
LILLERS	1-8-15	3	–	1	1	
"	2-8-15	6	–	–	–	
"	3-8-15	3	–	–	–	
"	4-8-15	4	–	–	–	
"	5-8-15	5	–	–	–	
"	6-8-15	11	16	–	–	
"	7-8-15	4	–	1	–	
"	8-8-15	1	23	–	–	
"	9-8-15	14	–	–	–	
"	10-8-15	11	–	–	–	
"	11-8-15	17	24	–	–	
"	12-8-15	5	39	–	–	
"	13-8-15	9	–	–	–	
"	14-8-15	8	–	–	–	
"	15-8-15	4	–	–	–	
"	16-8-15	4	23	–	–	
PACAUT	18-8-15	–	–	–	–	
"	19-8-15	6	–	–	–	
"	20-8-15	6	–	–	1	
BETHUNE	21-8-15	7	–	–	2	
"	22-8-15	2	–	–	–	
"	23-8-15	8	18	–	2	Includes 1 horse in foal
"	24-8-15	6	–	–	–	
"	25-8-15	4	–	–	1	
"	27-8-15	4	16	1	–	
"	29-8-15	1	–	–	–	
"	30-8-15	8	–	–	–	
"	31-8-15	3	–	–	–	
		164	159	3	7	

P. D. Carey
Capt.

7th Division

121
7049

No 12. Mobile Vety: Section

Vol VIII

Sept 15

✓

Instructions regarding War Diaries and Intelligence Summaries are contained in F. S. Regs., Part II. and the Staff Manual respectively. Title pages will be prepared in manuscript.

WAR DIARY
or
INTELLIGENCE SUMMARY

(Erase heading not required.)

12th Mobile Vet. Section.

Army Form C. 2118.

Hour, Date, Place	Summary of Events and Information	Remarks and references to Appendices
BETHUNE. 5-9-15	Received orders to take the section to FOUQUEREIL tomorrow. Tried to get a float to fetch a horse but was told that it was booked for 3 days ahead.	
FOUQUEREIL 6-9-15	Section at FOUQUEREIL in a good place. Rode out to find a collecting station. Decided to establish it at VERQUIGNEUL.	
7-9-15	Set the collecting station in a field adjoining the 14th R.H.A. A.C.	
9-9-15	Received 5 requests to send a float to collect animals at different places. This again shows how urgently a float is required for a M.V.S. Arranged with a [illegible] in billets to keep his float with the section.	
10-9-15	Received 22 horses for evacuation from the D.A.C. Requested that units & V.O.s of all other units to send 1 days rations whenever they send in an abnormal number of horses it being impossible to feed an unlimited number of horses.	
12-9-15	Collecting station removed to Le MARAIS. attached the men. horses to 37 Bde R.F.A. for rations.	
24-9-15	Found a place at Noyelles les MINES for an advanced collecting station.	
25-9-15	Received orders from A.D.V.S. to move the section to Le Marais. Later these orders were cancelled & I brought the section to LABOURCE	
26-9-15	Established an advanced collecting station at Noyelles les Mines. a great number of wounded horses were brought in.	
30-9-15	Brought the section back to BETHUNE established it in an [illegible] field near the Station. Kept the advanced collecting station at Noyelles. increased the number of men there by 2.	
	P. D. Carey. Capt A.V.C	

WAR DIARY
or
INTELLIGENCE SUMMARY

(Erase heading not required.)

Army Form C. 2118.

Instructions regarding War Diaries and Intelligence Summaries are contained in F. S. Regs., Part II. and the Staff Manual respectively. Title pages will be prepared in manuscript.

Hour, Date, Place	Summary of Events and Information: Admitted	Transferred	Died or Destroyed	Dissued(?)	Remarks and references to Appendices
1-9-15	1	–	–	1	
2 " "	–	16	2	1	
3 " "	9	–	–	–	
4 " "	7	16	2	–	
5 " "	4		–	1	
6 " "	1	–	–	–	
8 " "	5	–	1	–	
9 " "	2		–	2	
10 " "	39.	33.	–		
11 " "	32	–			
12 " "	27	40	4	–	
13 " "	5	–	1	1	
14 " "	14	–	–	–	
15 " "	5	24	–	–	
17 " "	19	–	–	–	
18 " "	5	20	1	–	
19 " "	3		1	–	
20 " "	7	–	–	–	
21	11				
22 " "	9	14	2	2	
23	6	–	1	1	
24	14	23	–	–	
25	12	8	–	–	
26	34	16	1	–	
27	16	27	–	2	
28	23	16	4	–	
29	7	3	2	–	
30	–	10	1	1	
Total	307	270	20	11	P. D. Carey Capt AVC

NO. 12 MOBILE VETERINARY SECTION 1915

1247 W 3299 200,000 (E) 8/14 J.B.C. & A. Forms/C. 2118/11.

WD

July – Oct 15

7th Division

2/7341

No 12 Mobile Vety: Section

Vol IX

Oct 15

✓

ans

Instructions regarding War Diaries and Intelligence Summaries are contained in F. S. Regs., Part II. and the Staff Manual respectively. Title pages will be prepared in manuscript.

WAR DIARY
or
INTELLIGENCE SUMMARY
(Erase heading not required.)

Army Form C. 2118.

12 Mobile Vet^y Section.

Hour, Date, Place	Summary of Events and Information	Remarks and references to Appendices
3-10-15	Established a collecting station at LE PRÉOL.	
7-10-15	Withdrew the collecting station from NOYELLES.	
15-10-15	Moved the section into a large stable in the Rue Gendarmerie.	
17-10-15	Withdrew the collecting station from Le Preol	
19-10-15	Found a farm at HAM en ARTOIS for the section, as the Division is moving back, sent out an advanced party	
20-10-15	Started for HAM at 10 o'clock with remainder of Section on the road got a wire from ADVS not to leave Bethune till further orders so immediately returned	
24-10-15	Received orders to move the section about 100 yds, as the place we are now in is not in our Divisional area. We are to share the same field as the 2^d Div: Mobile. This does not seem to me to be satisfactory from a Disciplinary point of view	
28-10-15	A.D.V.S went on leave, took over his duties	
29-10-15	A.D.V.S. 2^d Div: went on leave, took over his duties in addition	
30-10-15	Attended a conference of A.D.V.S. at Locon, held under & by order of the D.D.V.S following subjects were discussed (1) the advisability of giving lectures in Horsemastership during the winter to officers & men (2) Clipping horses.	
31-10-15	Inspected the 106 Bty carefully, found 2 cases of suspected mange so sent them into the Mobile for safety & confirmation.	
30-10-15	Collected a horse at VENDIN. that had been left by 28th Div. This animal had been absolutely starved, so assessed the rate at 5' per day.	

P. J. Carey Capt A.V.C.

Army Form C. 2118.

Instructions regarding War Diaries and Intelligence Summaries are contained in F. S. Regs., Part II. and the Staff Manual respectively. Title pages will be prepared in manuscript.

WAR DIARY
or
INTELLIGENCE SUMMARY

(Erase heading not required.)

12 Mobile Vet Section

Hour, Date, Place	Admitted	Transferred	Died or Destroyed	Returned
1.10.15	10	16		2
2	5			
3	13			1
4	1			
5	10	24	1	
6	4			
7	2			
8	8	16		
9	9			1
10	10			
12		13		
13	2			
14	5			1
15	3	16	1	
16	6			1
17	4			
18	5		1	
19	3			1
21	1	16	1	
22	3			
23	4			
24	3			1
26	2			
27	15			
28	1	8		
29	7	16		1
30	4	9		
31	6			
	146	134	4	9

P. D Carey Capt

7th Division

No. 12. Mob. Vet. Sec.

Nov

Vol X

121
7655

Instructions regarding War Diaries and Intelligence Summaries are contained in F. S. Regs., Part II. and the Staff Manual respectively. Title pages will be prepared in manuscript.

WAR DIARY
or
~~INTELLIGENCE SUMMARY~~

(Erase heading not required.) 12th Mobile Vet Section November

Army Form C. 2118.

Hour, Date, Place	Summary of Events and Information	Remarks and references to Appendices
Bethune 1-11-15	No 554. Sergt Goulthorpe joined for duty with the Section	
2-11-15.	Received a wire from D.D.V.S. saying that a case of glanders from the HQrs 2 Div. had been found at Abbeville, I was ordered to go into the matter. Wired for a [illegible] mallein.	
3-11-15	D.D.V.S came, went to the Section of 2nd Div but cannot trace the horse	
4-11-15	I inspected all the horses of the HQrs 2nd Div. & found them free from disease forwarded a report to this effect.	
	On hearing that the 11th Corps are probably going to leave Bethune. I went to the Town Major & persuaded him to reserve the place in 8th [illegible] for the Mobile Section, or at least for the 7th Div.	
7-11-15	A.D.V.S. returned from leave	
9-11-15	I go on leave to the 18th	
9-11-15	Capt Carey went on leave A.D.V.S takes over charge of Vet Mob Sect	
20-11-15	Capt G. M. Dawson appointed to take over command of Mob Sect	
21-11-15	Capt G. M. Dawson takes over Mob Sect.	
22-11-15	78 horses sent to Base hospital from 106th Bty 22nd Bde R.F.A. These were the horses taken over from the 28th Division, before it left the district. They were mange - suspected mange horses	
23-11-15	Great difficulty in securing float to bring in horses unable to move Only one available in the district	
26-11-15	Take over duties of Lieut Fox who proceeded on leave	
27-11-15	Had two horses sent to Section to-day suffering from rupture of eyeball This seems to be due to horses being secured by wire to the picket line	
29-11-15	Visited a section of Reserve Park affiliated to 1st Corps at present situated at OBLINGHEM.	G M Dawson Capt A.V.C

1247 W 3299 200,000 (E) 8/14 J.B.C. & A. Forms/C. 2118/11.

Instructions regarding War Diaries and Intelligence Summaries are contained in F. S. Regs., Part II. and the Staff Manual respectively. Title pages will be prepared in manuscript.

WAR DIARY
or
~~INTELLIGENCE~~ SUMMARY

(Erase heading not required.)

Army Form C. 2118.

Hour, Date, Place	Summary of Events and Information				Remarks and references to Appendices
	Admitted	Transferred	Died or Destroyed	Reissued	
1 – 11 – 15	6	15	–		
2 – " – "	9	–	–	–	
3 – " – "	5	–	–	–	
4 – " – "	3	15	–	–	
5 – " – "	4	–	–	–	
6 – " – "	3	–	–	–	
7 – " – "	10	8	–	–	
8 – " – "	9	8	–	–	
9 – " – "	2	11	–	–	
10 – " – "	1	–	–	–	
11 – " – "	7	–	–	–	
12 – " – "	1	–	–	–	
13 – " – "	7	8	–	–	
14 – " – "	30	–	–	–	
15 – " – "	11	18	–	–	
16 – " – "	21	16	2	–	
17 – " – "	25	24	–	–	
18 – " – "	11	36	–	1	
19 – " – "	11	15	–	1	
20 – " – "	4	7	–	–	
21 – " – "	3	78	–	–	
22 – " – "	85	21	–	–	
23 – " – "	14	7	–	–	
24 – " – "	7	9	–	–	
25 – " – "	–	–	–	–	
26 – " – "	3	–	–	–	
27 – " – "	10	3	–	–	
28 – " – "	7	11	–	–	
29 – " – "	7	9	1	–	
30 – " – "	11	8	–	–	

G. M. Dawson
Capt. A.V.C.

1247 W 3299 200,000 (E) 8/14 J.B.C. & A. Forms/C. 2118/11.

7th Div

7

12 Mob. Vet. Sec.

Dec

Vol. XI

121/7951

Instructions regarding War Diaries and Intelligence Summaries are contained in F. S. Regs., Part II. and the Staff Manual respectively. Title pages will be prepared in manuscript.

WAR DIARY

or

~~INTELLIGENCE SUMMARY~~

(Erase heading not required.)

Army Form C. 2118.

Hour, Date, Place	Summary of Events and Information	Remarks and references to Appendices
1st Dec 1915	Still in Bethune at Skating Rink. Collected two horses from LES HARISOIRS left by 2nd Gordons. Had to destroy one	
2nd Dec 1915	[redacted] Mobile Section 33rd Division came in to Bethune to-day & settled down in Skating Rink.	
4th Dec 1915	Handed over 4 horses to No 3 Mob Vet Sect on account of this Section moving to LE CORNET BRASSART near BERGUETTE. On arriving there found billets occupied by the 2nd Highland Field Coy. Obtained possession after 4 hours wait.	
5th Dec 1915	Rode to HAM-en-ARTOIS & arranged with O.C. 23rd Mob. Sect. to send any cases I had to him. Superintended entraining of horses at BERGUETTE	← Corpl. DAVIS arrives from No 3 Vet Hospital Boulogne.
6th Dec 1915	Sent 1 horse to No 23 Mob. Vet. Sect. Superintended entraining of horses at BERGUETTE	
7th Dec 1915	O.C. 23 Mob Vet. Sect. arranged to collect 2 horses left by Artillery at LAMBRES. Entrained Section for new Area without mishap. Left BERGUETTE at 1-30 P.M. arrived at PONT REMY at 10-30 without accident. Parked Section in a field near Station for the night. Superintended the detrainment of horses in succeeding trains.	← Corpl. Kerby proceeded to No 3 Vet Hospital BOULOGNE
8th Dec 1915	Still busy detraining. Remained all day at PONT. REMY. Stn. until the last Divisional horse had been detrained. In morning sent Section to BELLOY, where it went into Billets. Had to leave two horses billeted with the French people at Hotel de la Gare, PONT. REMY. Rode over to BELLOY in evening	
9th Dec 1915	Got Section comfortably settled.	
10th Dec 1915	Rode to PICQUIGNY to see A.D.V.S. about float. Section is very much handicapped without a horse-float now that the Divisional Area is so wide. Took over Vet Charge of 20th INF. BDE & 95th Field Coy Royal Engineers.	
11th Dec 1915	Received two cases of punctured eyeball due to tying horses up with wire. Stricter measures should be taken in this matter	
12th Dec 1915	Went to PONT REMY with A.D.V.S to see the two horses left behind. Found that the A.D.V.S. 36th DIVISION had already evacuated them.	
14th Dec 1915	Collected two horses left by 24th Division. One with Skin Disease from PISSY and one Laminitis case from FERRIERES. Put down some standings for horses in lines in Section to-day.	

Instructions regarding War Diaries and Intelligence Summaries are contained in F. S. Regs., Part II. and the Staff Manual respectively. Title pages will be prepared in manuscript.

WAR DIARY

or

~~INTELLIGENCE SUMMARY~~

(Erase heading not required.)

Army Form C. 2118.

Hour, Date, Place	Summary of Events and Information	Remarks and references to Appendices
19th Dec 1915	Arranged with M. Ray, HANGEST for him to leave his float at section ~~ch~~ return for his receiving the dead horses	
20th Dec 1915	95th Field Coy R.E put up shelters for sick horses, cook house & Latrine. Still occupied putting down standings for the horses	
26th Dec 1915	Sent two horses to Abbatoir at Amiens. Suffering from Necrosis. It is a singular fact that nearly every case of Necrotic heels to this Section comes from the Artillery.	
	G.W. Dawson Capt A.V.C	

1247 W 3299 200,000 (E) 8/14 J.B.C. & A. Forms/C. 2118/11.

Army Form C. 2118.

Instructions regarding War Diaries and Intelligence Summaries are contained in F. S. Regs., Part II. and the Staff Manual respectively. Title pages will be prepared in manuscript.

WAR DIARY
or
INTELLIGENCE SUMMARY
(Erase heading not required.)

Hour, Date, Place	Summary of Events and Information				Remarks and references to Appendices
	Admitted	Transferred	Died & Destroyed	Reissued	
1 - 12 - 15	10	18	1	1	
2 - 12 - 15	7	13		1	
3 - 12 - 15	4	4			
4 - 12 - 15	1	1			
5 - 12 - 15	—	2			
6 - 12 - 15	—	2			
7 - 12 - 15	2	—			
8 - 12 - 15	1	—			
9 - 12 - 15	8	8			
10 - 12 - 15	3	7			
11 - 12 - 15		—			
12 - 12 - 15	1	—	1		
13 - 12 - 15	1	—			
14 - 12 - 15	2	10			
15 - 12 - 15	1	—	1		
16 - 12 - 15		—			
17 - 12 - 15	2	5		1	
18 - 12 - 15	1	—	2		
19 - 12 - 15	4	—			
20 - 12 - 15	3	—			
21 - 12 - 15	—	8	1		
22 - 12 - 15	1	5			
23 - 12 - 15	—	—			
24 - 12 - 15	—				
25 - 12 - 15					
26 - 12 - 15	—				
27 - 12 - 15	3				
28 - 12 - 15	4				
29 - 12 - 15	4				
30 - 12 - 15	—				
31 - 12 - 15	8				
	85	64	6		J. W. Dawson Capt A.V.C

1247 W 3299 200,000 (E) 8/14 J.B.C. & A. Forms/C. 2118/11.

Instructions regarding War Diaries and Intelligence Summaries are contained in F. S. Regs., Part II. and the Staff Manual respectively. Title pages will be prepared in manuscript.

WAR DIARY
or
INTELLIGENCE SUMMARY

(Erase heading not required.)

Army Form C. 2118.

Hour, Date, Place	Summary of Events and Information	Remarks and references to Appendices
1st Feb 1916 BELLOY	Division on the move Clearing out all the horses of the Units unable to march with them.	
5th Feb "	Left BELLOY. Sur SOMME Two days trek in front of us. Halted at S.T. GRATIEN for the night	
6th Feb "	Set out for MERICOURT l'ABBE arriving there in the evening take over billet vacated by 30th mobile Section. Find this Section very handy, although the accomodation is limited, being close to rail head	
19th Feb 1916	A Chestnut Gelding belonging to Hd. Qrs 22nd Bde R.F.A. reacted to the Palpebral test for Glanders at 22 Vet Hospital. This animal had been tested twice in this Division, firstly with the Palpebral ~~test~~ and later with Subcutaneous Cervical test.	
20th Feb 1916	Find the majority of horses being sent in here, suffer badly from lice. This is due, in my opinion to the extreme difficulty of thoroughly cleaning the unnecessarily long coats of the horses. Had the horses of this Division been clipped last September, there would have been nothing like the amount of skin affections now raging.	
	J M Dawson Capt. A.V.C	

…R DIARY

or

INTELLIGENCE SUMMARY

(Erase heading not required.)

Army Form C. 2118.

Instructions regarding War Diaries and Intelligence Summaries are contained in F. S. Regs., Part II. and the Staff Manual respectively. Title pages will be prepared in manuscript.

Hour, Date, Place	Summary of Events and Information: Admitted	Transferred	Died. Destroyed	Reissued	Remarks and references to Appendices
1	8	–	–	–	
2	6	–	–	–	
3	3	–	–	–	
4	–	20	–	1	
5	–	–	–	–	
6	–	–	–	–	
7	5	–	–	–	
8	7	–	–	–	
9	3	11	–	2	
10	2	–	–	–	
11	4	–	–	–	
12	1	–	–	–	
13	6	–	–	–	
14	4	18	–	1	
15	7	–	–	–	
16	3	–	–	–	
17	5	–	–	–	
18	1	15	–	–	
19	4	–	–	–	
20	1	–	–	–	
21	10	–	–	–	
22	8	–	–	–	
23	1	16	1	/	
24	9	–	–	–	
25	4	–	–	–	
26	–	–	–	–	
27	4	22	–	/	
28	5	–	–	/	
29	9	–	–	–	
	120	102	1	4	

[illegible signature]
Capt. A.V.C.

Instructions regarding War Diaries and Intelligence Summaries are contained in F. S. Regs., Part II. and the Staff Manual respectively. Title pages will be prepared in manuscript.

WAR DIARY
or
INTELLIGENCE SUMMARY.
(Erase heading not required.)

Army Form C. 2118.

7

Vol X 13

Place	Date	Hour	Summary of Events and Information	Remarks and references to Appendices
			No: 12 Mobile Vet. Section	
			War Diary	
			of	
			Captain J M Dawson	
			AVC	
			From 1st to 31st March 1916	

2353 Wt. W2544/1454 700,000 5/15 D. D. & L. A.D.S.S./Forms/C. 2118.

Instructions regarding War Diaries and Intelligence Summaries are contained in F. S. Regs., Part II. and the Staff Manual respectively. Title pages will be prepared in manuscript.

WAR DIARY
or
INTELLIGENCE SUMMARY.
(Erase heading not required.)

Army Form C. 2118.

Place	Date	Hour	Summary of Events and Information	Remarks and references to Appendices
	1 March 1916. to 31st March 1916		A rather uneventful month, Two hundred and [illegible] horses have been admitted and about 130 have been evacuated to Base and about a dozen have been returned cured. I have had to destroy several animals during the month, including one case of Rupture and a bad case of Quittor.	
			The standings have been much improved since we arrived last month, the weather however has been very bad and it is still difficult to keep some of the standings "solid". Some of the horses I have been able to put under cover. I have had several units to look after in addition to my work as O/C of the Section. The following is a summary of admissions, evacuations, [illegible] etc during this month [illegible]	

2353 Wt. W2544/1454 700,000 5/15 D. D. & L. A.D.S.S./Forms/C. 2118.

Instructions regarding War Diaries and Intelligence Summaries are contained in F. S. Regs., Part II. and the Staff Manual respectively. Title pages will be prepared in manuscript.

WAR DIARY
or
INTELLIGENCE SUMMARY
(Erase heading not required.)

Army Form C. 2118.

Hour, Date, Place	Summary of Events and Information				Remarks and references to Appendices
	Admitted	Transferred Sick	Destroyed	Cured	
1 March 1916.	5				
2 "	16				
3 "	2	24		1	
4 "	5			1	
5 "	3			2 1	
6 "	3		1		
7 "	12				
8	5	25			
9 "	3			1	
10	5				
11	7				
12	1				
13	5		2		
14	6	22			
15	8			1	
16	3			1	
17	12	22	1		
18	2				
19.	4				
20	22	23		1	
21	8				
	137	116	4	9	

1247 W 3299 200,000 (E) 8/14 J.B.C. & A. Forms/C. 2118/11.

Instructions regarding War Diaries and Intelligence Summaries are contained in F. S. Regs., Part II. and the Staff Manual respectively. Title pages will be prepared in manuscript.

WAR DIARY
or
INTELLIGENCE SUMMARY
(Erase heading not required.)

Army Form C. 2118.

Hour, Date, Place	Summary of Events and Information								Remarks and references to Appendices
		137		116		4		9	
22 March 1916	Admitted	7.	Transf Sick	17	Destroyed		Cured		
23 "		3							
24 "		11						1	
25		4						1	
26		9			Died 1				
27		4			Destroyed 1			1	
28		7		17					
29		4							
31		15.							
	Totals	201		150		6		12	G.H. Dawson Capt AVC

1247 W 3299 200,000 (E) 8/14 J.B.C. & A. Forms/C. 2118/11.

Instructions regarding War Diaries and Intelligence Summaries are contained in F. S. Regs., Part II. and the Staff Manual respectively. Title pages will be prepared in manuscript.

WAR DIARY
or
INTELLIGENCE SUMMARY.
(Erase heading not required.)

Army Form C. 2118.

Vol 14

Place	Date	Hour	Summary of Events and Information	Remarks and references to Appendices
			No 12. Mobile Veterinary Section	
			War Diary	
			of	
			Captain J M Dawson	
			AVC	
			From 1st to 30th April 1916	

2353 Wt. W2544/1454 700,000 5/15 D. D. & L. A.D.S.S./Forms/C. 2118.

Instructions regarding War Diaries and Intelligence Summaries are contained in F. S. Regs., Part II. and the Staff Manual respectively. Title pages will be prepared in manuscript.

WAR DIARY
or
INTELLIGENCE SUMMARY.

(Erase heading not required.)

Army Form C. 2118.

Place	Date	Hour	Summary of Events and Information	Remarks and references to Appendices
	1st April 1916 to 30th April 1916		Like last month, April has been an eventful one. I have had much to do in the [illegible] lines and attending to other units under my veterinary charge; and I find it as much as I can do to get round. In [illegible] 183 animals have been admitted this month, 96 evacuated, [illegible] 8 destroyed & 5 returned as cured. Several of those destroyed were through bad backs, a large proportion of these admissions are suffering from [illegible] injuries. There are also a good many debility cases, one exceptionally bad case of debility from [illegible] had to be destroyed. The weather still continues bad and the standings where there are any [illegible] soft making it bad for the horses. The following is a summary of admissions, evacuations & [illegible]	

2353 Wt. W2544/1454 700,000 5/15 D. D. & L. A.D.S.S./Forms/C. 2118.

Instructions regarding War Diaries and Intelligence Summaries are contained in F. S. Regs., Part II. and the Staff Manual respectively. Title pages will be prepared in manuscript.

WAR DIARY
or
INTELLIGENCE SUMMARY
(Erase heading not required.)

Army Form C. 2118.

Hour, Date, Place	Summary of Events and Information					Remarks and references to Appendices
1 Apl 1916	Admitted 4	Transferred	[illegible]	Discharged	V Cases	
2	3					
3	2					
4	6	15				
5	6					
6	6			2		
7	6	15				
8	1				1	
9	3					
10	11					
11	3			Air 1		
12	4				1	
13	5					
14	2	17		1		
15	2					
16	2					
17	2					
18	1					
19	14			1	1	
20	12				1	
21	8	25				
22	13					
23	8					
24	10					
25	7					
26	14	13		2		
27	4				1	
28	11	11				
29	7					
30	7					
	183	96		8	5	

1247 W 3299 200,000 (E) 8/14 J.B.C. & A. Forms/C. 2118/11.

Army Form C. 2118.

Vol 15

Instructions regarding War Diaries and Intelligence Summaries are contained in F. S. Regs., Part II. and the Staff Manual respectively. Title pages will be prepared in manuscript.

WAR DIARY
or
INTELLIGENCE SUMMARY
(Erase heading not required.)

Hour, Date, Place	Summary of Events and Information	Remarks and references to Appendices
	No. 12 Mobile Veterinary Section	
	War Diary	
	of	
	Captain J M Dawson	
	A.V.C.	
	From 1st to 31st May 1916.	

No. 12 MOBILE VETERINARY SECTION 7 AUG. 1916

Instructions regarding War Diaries and Intelligence Summaries are contained in F. S. Regs., Part II. and the Staff Manual respectively. Title pages will be prepared in manuscript.

WAR DIARY
or
INTELLIGENCE SUMMARY
(Erase heading not required.)

Army Form C. 2118.

Hour, Date, Place	Summary of Events and Information	Remarks and references to Appendices
Merricourt. 3 May 1916	Sent float to 91 Inf Bde Machine Gun Sec. Bray to convey 1 horse to Mobile Section.	
4 May 1916	Sent float to 21 Field Ambulance. Morlancourt to convey 1 horse to Mobile Section	
8 May 1916.	Sent float to 22 Bde RFA Ammunition Column Morlancourt to convey 1 horse to Mobile Section.	
19th May 1916	Sent float to Morlancourt for a horse belonging to F Batt 1st Bde RHA which had been badly burned	
20th May 1916	Sent Float to Bois de Tailly for a horse of 20th Infy Bde 2nd Gordons another bad case of burns	
23rd May 1916	Sent Float for horse of 91st Machine Gun Section at Bois de Tailly which I found to be suffering from partial Radial Paralysis	
26th May 1916	Sent Float to Bois de Tailly for horse of 1/4 Cameron Highlanders Lothian Bde	
30th May 1916	Sent Float to 22 Bde R F A. 10th Batt at Morlancourt to bring in a horse	

Army Form C. 2118.

Instructions regarding War Diaries and Intelligence Summaries are contained in F. S. Regs., Part II. and the Staff Manual respectively. Title pages will be prepared in manuscript.

WAR DIARY
or
INTELLIGENCE SUMMARY

(Erase heading not required.)

Hour, Date, Place	Summary of Events and Information: Admitted	Transferred	Died & Destroyed	Re-issued	Remarks and references to Appendices
1 - 5 - 16 Morricourt	4	–	–	–	
2 - 5 - 16	10	–	–	1	
3 - 5 - 16	2	16	–	2	
4 - 5 - 16	–	–	–	–	
5 - 5 - 16	8	–	–	–	
6 - 5 - 16	2	–	4	–	
7 - 5 - 16	2	–	–	–	
8 - 5 - 16	3	–	–	1	
9 - 5 - 16	2	–			
10 - 5 - 16	1	–	–	–	
11 - 5 - 16	1	25		10	
12 5 16	9		1		
13 5 16	1				
14 5 16	3			1	
15 5 16	21				
16 5 16	7	39		2	
18 5 16	3			3	
19 5 16	9			9	
20 5 16	6				
21 5 16	28			2	
22 5 16	7	31	1		
23 5 16	18				
24 5 16	4	31	2	6	
25 5 16	1			1	
26 5 16	5			1	
27 5 16	6				

1247 W 3299 200,000 (E) 8/14 J.B.C. & A. Forms/C. 2118/11.

Instructions regarding War Diaries and Intelligence Summaries are contained in F. S. Regs., Part II. and the Staff Manual respectively. Title pages will be prepared in manuscript.

WAR DIARY
or
INTELLIGENCE SUMMARY
(Erase heading not required.)

Army Form C. 2118.

Hour, Date, Place	Summary of Events and Information				Remarks and references to Appendices
	Admitted	Transferred	Died or destroyed	Returned	
28 6 16	3				
29 5 16	6			2	
30 5 16	5	25.		2	
31 5 16	2			1	

G M Dawson
Captain A V C
O/C 12th [illegible]

1247 W 3299 200,000 (E) 8/14 J.B.C. & A. Forms/C. 2118/11.

Instructions regarding War Diaries and Intelligence Summaries are contained in F. S. Regs., Part II. and the Staff Manual respectively. Title pages will be prepared in manuscript.

WAR DIARY
or
INTELLIGENCE SUMMARY
(Erase heading not required.)

Army Form C. 2118.

Vol 16

Hour, Date, Place	Summary of Events and Information	Remarks and references to Appendices
	No: 12. Mobile Veterinary Section.	
	War Diary	
	– of –	
	Captain J M Dawson AVC	
	From 1st to 30th June 1916.	

Instructions regarding War Diaries and Intelligence Summaries are contained in F. S. Regs., Part II. and the Staff Manual respectively. Title pages will be prepared in manuscript.

WAR DIARY
or
INTELLIGENCE SUMMARY
(Erase heading not required.)

Army Form C. 2118.

Hour, Date, Place	Summary of Events and Information	Remarks and references to Appendices
2 June 1916,	Sent Float for horse of 2 Indian Cavalry Division which had been badly kicked	
3	Sent float for horse of 3 Co A.S.C. 34 Divl Train suffering from [illegible]	
4	Sent float for horse of 14 Bde R.H.A. T. Batt[y] suffering from Kick O.H.	
7	Sent float to Steenvoorde for horse of 19 Cheshires a Laminitis case	
10	Sent float for a Quittor case from 21 Manchesters 91st Inf Bde	
	Also to 35 Bde R.F.A. 12 Batt for horse with [illegible]	
14	Sent float for horse of 4 Co 7 Div[l] Train Kick N.H.	
15	Sent float for horse of 14 Bde R.H.A. Kick N Hock	
16	Sent float to Canadian [illegible] Batt[n] a case of Pricked heel	
18	Sent float to 14th R.H.A. for horse with punctured foot (P.W.N)	
	Also for a case Kick both belonging to "T" Batt[y]	
19	Sent out float to 1/2 Lancs [illegible] Batt R.G.A. [illegible] [illegible] N [illegible] [illegible] Bas de [illegible] with A.D.V.S. whose collecting station was to be	

1247 W 3299 200,000 (E) 8/14 J.B.C. & A. Forms/C. 2118/11.

Army Form C. 2118.

WAR DIARY
or
INTELLIGENCE SUMMARY
(Erase heading not required.)

Instructions regarding War Diaries and Intelligence Summaries are contained in F. S. Regs., Part II. and the Staff Manual respectively. Title pages will be prepared in manuscript.

Hour, Date, Place	Summary of Events and Information	Remarks and references to Appendices
21 June 1916	Sent float to 9 Bde Train ASC Co for a case of P.U. [illegible]	
24 "	Sent float to 20 Inf Bde Transport Section Sick [illegible] horse. Two N.C.Os and 18 men have arrived to assist at [illegible]	
26	Sent float to 14 Batt RHA for Sick case [illegible] to 130 Bty Batt RHG Contused Wound Elbow	
29	One NCO and five men have been sent up from No 7 [illegible] Hospital Forges Les Eaux by instructions of DVS. These men will assist as conducting party in evacuation of sick and injured animals. The men have been placed with the Divisional Collecting Station [illegible] [illegible] [illegible] placed in position a few days ago	

1247 W 3299 200,000 (E) 8/14 J.B.C. & A. Forms/C. 2118/11.

Instructions regarding War Diaries and Intelligence Summaries are contained in F. S. Regs., Part II. and the Staff Manual respectively. Title pages will be prepared in manuscript.

WAR DIARY
or
INTELLIGENCE SUMMARY
(Erase heading not required.)

Army Form C. 2118.

Hour, Date, Place	Admitted	Transferred Sick	Cured	Died or destroyed	Remarks and references to Appendices
1 June 1916.	3		8		
2	19		6	2	
3	1	23	4		
4	2		3		
5	2			6	
6	4				
7	2				
8	5		2		
9	9				
10	5		1		
11	5				
12	14		6		
13	9	16	2		
14	8		3		
15	6				
16	6		4		
17	11				
18	15	33	5		
19	17			2	
20	16		1	1	
21	6	43		2	
22	12		1		
23	13		1		
24	8	46	4		
25	8		3		
26	16		4		
27	8	1	6		
28	9	43	7	2	
29	10				
30	13		4		
	257	205	75	15	

J W Dawson
Captain A.V.C.
O/C 1st Mobile Vet. [illegible]

Army Form C. 2118.

Instructions regarding War Diaries and Intelligence Summaries are contained in F. S. Regs., Part II. and the Staff Manual respectively. Title pages will be prepared in manuscript.

WAR DIARY
or
INTELLIGENCE SUMMARY
(Erase heading not required.)

Vol 17

Hour, Date, Place	Summary of Events and Information	Remarks and references to Appendices
	12th Mobile Vet Section War Diary – of – Captain J. M. Dawson A.V.C From 1st to 31st July 1916.	

1247 W 3299 200,000 (E) 8/14 J.B.C. & A. Forms/C. 2118/11.

Instructions regarding War Diaries and Intelligence Summaries are contained in F. S. Regs., Part II. and the Staff Manual respectively. Title pages will be prepared in manuscript.

WAR DIARY
or
INTELLIGENCE SUMMARY
(Erase heading not required.)

Army Form C. 2118.

Hour, Date, Place	Summary of Events and Information	Remarks and references to Appendices
1. July 1916. to 5th	Twenty eight animals passed through the Collecting Station. The advanced collecting Station has been withdrawn this morning (5th) the Division having gone back to rest, about 40 animals have been admitted casualties though [illegible] very small, I have evacuated 60 horses between these dates.	
6th to 10th	Busy at Station and at Station [illegible] sick horses, find I have not sufficient men, 24 horses have been admitted between these dates	
11th	Have opened a Collecting Station at Becordel, placing one man there, I have my horses [illegible] at the Station	
12th to 15th	About 60 animals have been admitted since the 10th but the majority come from other Divisions than the 7th. I find it is necessary that more men should be placed at the advanced Station so have sent over four more men which leaves me rather short at the Station	

1247 W 3299 200,000 (E) 8/14 J.B.C. & A. Forms/C. 2118/11.

Instructions regarding War Diaries and Intelligence Summaries are contained in F. S. Regs., Part II. and the Staff Manual respectively. Title pages will be prepared in manuscript.

WAR DIARY
or
INTELLIGENCE SUMMARY
(Erase heading not required.)

Army Form C. 2118.

Hour, Date, Place	Summary of Events and Information	Remarks and references to Appendices
	I have been called upon to collect so many float cases that the single horse drawn float is not near sufficient to meet requirements, I am receiving horses from five or six other Divisions, the float I have is very heavy & being built very low find it a most difficult mode of conveyance on roads in the neighbourhood which have been badly cut up owing to so much heavy traffic, a double horse float (i.e. taking two sick animals) is what is really required at a time like this. A horse drawn float is only capable sometimes of getting in more than one case. Fifty seven horses passed thro' the Collecting Station yesterday	
19th July	I have received an addition of 2 NCOs & 18 men from No 8 Vety Hospital to assist as Conducting Party & 2 NCOs & 8 men from 23 Mobile Section	

1247 W 3299 200,000 (E) 8/14 J.B.C. & A. Forms/C. 2118/11.

Instructions regarding War Diaries and Intelligence Summaries are contained in F. S. Regs., Part II. and the Staff Manual respectively. Title pages will be prepared in manuscript.

WAR DIARY
or
INTELLIGENCE SUMMARY
(Erase heading not required.)

Army Form C. 2118.

Hour, Date, Place	Summary of Events and Information	Remarks and references to Appendices
20 July 1916	I hear it is possible that the Section will move to [illegible] as the Division is going back to rest. A.D.V.S. informs me I must remain for a time but to send some men under charge of Capt Fox(?) A.V.C. to act as a Branch of the Mobile to go with the Infantry. And seven men to do this.	
21st July to 31st July 1916	Have been very busy at the Section and also superintending the evacuation of sick animals of the Section & the [illegible] of [illegible] horses and supply of [illegible] horses for the various Mobile Sections in the neighbourhood. A large number of animals have been admitted and transferred [illegible] [illegible] the [illegible]	

[illegible signature]
Capt A.V.C.
O/C 12 Mobile Vety Sec

P.T.O.

1247 W 3299 200,000 (E) 8/14 J.B.C. & A. Forms/C. 2118/11.

Instructions regarding War Diaries and Intelligence Summaries are contained in F. S. Regs., Part II. and the Staff Manual respectively. Title pages will be prepared in manuscript.

WAR DIARY

or

INTELLIGENCE SUMMARY

(Erase heading not required.)

Army Form C. 2118.

Hour, Date, Place	Summary of Events and Information								Remarks and references to Appendices
1 July 1916	Officers admitted	15	Transferred Sick	39	Cured	2	Died & destroyed		
2 " "		13							
3 " "		11				1			
4 " "		1		21					
5 "		7							
6		4				1			
7 "		4							
8 "		6						1	
9		7							
10		3							
11 "		11							
12		10		27					
13		8							
14		12				1			
15 "		30		47		2			
16		37				1			
17		18				2			
18		13		44					
19		20		34		8			
20		11		1					
21		24		23		6			
22		12				1			
23		22		36		1			
24		9				1			
25		14		37					
26		5							
27		20							
28		9		20					
29		6		11					
31		3		3					
		363		343		22		7	

1247 W 3299 200,000 (E) 8/14 J.B.C. & A. Forms/C. 2118/11.

Army Form C. 2118.

Instructions regarding War Diaries and Intelligence Summaries are contained in F. S. Regs., Part II. and the Staff Manual respectively. Title pages will be prepared in manuscript.

WAR DIARY
or
INTELLIGENCE SUMMARY.
(Erase heading not required.)

12 Mob Vet Section
Vol 18

Place	Date	Hour	Summary of Events and Information	Remarks and references to Appendices
			Confidential	
			War Diary	
			of	
			Captain J M Dawson A.V.C.	
			O/C 12 Mobile Section 7th Div	
			From 1st to 31st Augt 1916.	

2353 Wt. W2544/1454 700,000 5/15 D. D. & L. A.D.S.S./Forms/C. 2118.

Army Form C. 2118.

WAR DIARY
or
INTELLIGENCE SUMMARY.
(*Erase heading not required.*)

Instructions regarding War Diaries and Intelligence Summaries are contained in F. S. Regs., Part II. and the Staff Manual respectively. Title pages will be prepared in manuscript.

Place	Date	Hour	Summary of Events and Information	Remarks and references to Appendices
1916 August	1st		Busy at Section today, Picked out a number of animals for evacuation	
"	2nd		Arranging to evacuate sick horses tomorrow. I can scarce find men sufficient to meet demands from the various mobiles for conducting parties, great advantage being taken of the present arrangements, mobiles frequently send in animals, the previous night, and when under orders to move leave them on my hands to evacuate, on several occasions I have even had to prepare descriptive rolls for animals sent in, and affix labels, they having been sent in without either. [illegible]	
"	3rd		Evacuated sick horses to-day and attended to entrainment of horses of several mobiles, a bad case of rough shunting occurred at the station this evening, one truck being completely smashed in, one of 8 animals got its leg thro' the bottom of the truck, and when the latter was brought to a standstill the animal with one other was extricated from beneath the waggon, all eight horses had to be returned to section, no other truck being available to take them on that night.	
"	4		Took all available men of Section to Heilly where they were inspected by Fourth Army Commander, (with the Divisional Artillery and 91st Field Ambulance) a short address was given by the General to the troops present but from where we stood scarce a sentence could be heard — my men were much disappointed at this, the march to Heilly	

2353 Wt. W2544/1454 700,000 5/15 D. D. & L. A.D.S.S./Forms/C. 2118.

Instructions regarding War Diaries and Intelligence Summaries are contained in F. S. Regs., Part II. and the Staff Manual respectively. Title pages will be prepared in manuscript.

WAR DIARY
or
INTELLIGENCE SUMMARY.
(Erase heading not required.)

Army Form C. 2118.

Place	Date	Hour	Summary of Events and Information	Remarks and references to Appendices
August	1916		and back and the waiting about, took up the greater portion of the day. Evacuated 12 horses	
	5th		Attending to work of Station	
	6th		Superintending entrainment of sick horses at Station. A horse extended for evacuation died rather suddenly at the Station. I held a post mortem examination on the animal and found cause of death to be Enteritis. The A.D.V.S. inspected the animals in the Station to day and conferred with me regarding certain animals considered fit to go out as remounts to Infantry Units. One of the men attached – Pte Rodmore received a nasty kick whilst feeding up this evening. I think it will be advisable for him to go into Hospital. Some bad tempered animals pass thro' the station. I find too, that a good many horses admitted resent any attempt to touch their heads, and in some instances it is difficult to adjust their head collars or groom their heads. It is most noticeable and appears to me to be nothing more or less than great nervousness on the horses part caused in my belief by having been continually thrashed for the least thing on the head & nose by men who have had charge of them in their respective units. It seems to me I regret to say a rather common punishment inflicted by thoughtless men for the least restiveness or misbehaviour on the horse's part.	
	7th		I evacuated 52 sick horses to day. The majority of these were cases of debility sent in the A.D.V.S. instructions from Divisional Artillery. Made full report of case of [illegible] happening at Station in 3 [illegible] for D.D.V.S.'s information. The [illegible] was taken from the Sergeant in charge of Conducting party on day in question and signed by him.	

2353 Wt. W2544/1454 700,000 5/15 D. D. & L. A.D.S.S./Forms/C. 2118.

Instructions regarding War Diaries and Intelligence Summaries are contained in F. S. Regs., Part II. and the Staff Manual respectively. Title pages will be prepared in manuscript.

WAR DIARY
or
INTELLIGENCE SUMMARY.
(Erase heading not required.)

Army Form C. 2118.

Place	Date	Hour	Summary of Events and Information	Remarks and references to Appendices
	Aug 1916	8th	Engaged at Station Superintending evacuation of Sick Horses for Mobile Sections	
		9th	ditto ditto	
"		10th	Entraining Sick horses at Railhead. Have had a visit from DDVS and ADVS [illegible] Arrangements were eventually made for attached men to be returned to their respective hospitals, and horses offered by ADVS were sent to various Mobiles informing them that collecting parties would not be available after tomorrow. Evacuated 13 Sick cases	
"		11th	Entraining sick horses at Railhead. I understand Divisional Headquarters were at Bellemont (adjoining village) but for short time only. Received a number of animals from 12 Batt 35 RFA sent in by order of ADVS mostly debility cases and unfits for artillery work. Evacuated ten sick horses today = all debility cases	
"		12th	Superintending entrainment of sick horses at Station.	
"		13th	There is a possibility of the Section moving to Bellemont so I understand. [illegible] Section	
		14th	I have had the DDVS to see me today. DAQMG desires to know what animals of any were in Section, fit to receive as remounts, prepared a list and sent to him. Also picked out a number of horses for early evacuation	
		15th	Evacuated 40 Sick Animals	
"		16th	A conference of ADVS's with DDVS was held at the Section this afternoon. I have taken over, in addition to the work of the Section veterinary charge of [illegible], RE HQrs, 7th Signals, 24 Manchesters and 21st Field Ambulance, all at Bellemont.	

Army Form C. 2118.

Instructions regarding War Diaries and Intelligence Summaries are contained in F. S. Regs., Part II. and the Staff Manual respectively. Title pages will be prepared in manuscript.

WAR DIARY
or
INTELLIGENCE SUMMARY.
(Erase heading not required.)

Place	Date	Hour	Summary of Events and Information	Remarks and references to Appendices
Augst	1916	17th	Saw the A.D.V.S. D.D.R. also visited the Section inspected animals for casting on account of Vice, picked out three for casting and arranging to evacuate same (See * 19th below)	
"		18.	Sent float to Corbie (in response to wire) for Major Luckett's Charger (A.P.M. Corbie). Great difficulty was experienced in collection owing to insufficient address being given as to where the horse was to be found. It is a pity that greater care is not taken by V.Os to give a more explicit address when sending for a float, it frequently occurs that the float is sent out to some vague address and great time is wasted in searching for injured animals, instances have occurred where the float has returned without finding any trace of the animal and a second journey has had to be taken	
"		19	Visited by A.D.V.S., going through inspecting and picking out cases in Section for evacuation to Hospital, (* I have had to destroy an animal belonging to 7th Suffolks (3rd Division) owing to fracture of Tibia O.F., informed A.D.V.S. 3 Div.) A case "Stricture of Urethra" died this evening — 7th B.A.C.	
		20	Evacuated 33 horses to-day 30 sick and 3 cast by D.D.R. on 17th inst, Labels supplied for evacuation of animals are most difficult to write on, except the white labels (Medical) the Red (Specific cases) and Green (Surgical) are unfit for filling up in Ink and copying Ink pencil does not show up sufficiently and if wet runs and becomes unreadable. It has always been the same with these labels & it seems extraordinary that up to the present no improvement has been made in this respect. The new labels just in are worse if anything than previous issues	
"		21	Arranged for, and evacuated sick animals of 29th Mobile Section. This Section is moving at short notice, A.D.V.S. visited me today	

2353 Wt. W2544/1454 700,000 5/15 D. D. & L. A.D.S.S./Forms/C. 2118.

Army Form C. 2118.

Instructions regarding War Diaries and Intelligence Summaries are contained in F. S. Regs., Part II. and the Staff Manual respectively. Title pages will be prepared in manuscript.

WAR DIARY
or
INTELLIGENCE SUMMARY.
(Erase heading not required.)

Place	Date	Hour	Summary of Events and Information	Remarks and references to Appendices
1916	Aug	22	Sent Float for Horse of 22 Bde RFA D6 suffering from Sprained Tendon. NF	
	"	23	At Railhead with DAQMG and ADVS assisting unloading & of Remounts which had been sent up. Had to remove greater portion of these animals to section to await collection by units for which intended, Subsequently issued the horses to the units and notified DAQMG I had done so	
	"	24	Examined animals admitted to section & picked out a number of cases for Hospital	
	"	25	Evacuated 16 horses today. Visited by ADVO. went thro' a list of animals issued from my section for past two months, Sent Float to 14 RHA F Batt for horse injured by Gunshot (Shrapnel) ? Shoulder	
	"	26	ADVS informs me that I must have men ready for advance collecting station tomorrow. Subsequently received from him written instructions to this effect, men to start tomorrow morning	
	"	27	Six men left this morning for a point near Fricourt where I am opening an advance collecting station. Evacuated 17 sick horses today, Visited advance collecting station this afternoon. The ADVS has been over to see me this morning. His office is still at Ribemont	
		28	Time taken up by ordinary work of section. Have been visited by ADVS.	
		29	Went to visit 21 Field Ambulance. The other units under my charge have moved, visited Field Cashier	
		30	Sent Float to Corbie for Horse belonging to 1st Prisoner of War Co ASC PWN visited by ADVS	
		31	I have had to destroy an animal of 35 Bde RFA 12 Batt. A case of Tortilanitis. ADR has inspected three animals for casting & made arrangements for this to be done. Intend to evacuate some sick horses tomorrow & shall dispatch the three cast at same time. 251 Sick animals have been admitted during this month, 197 have been evacuated sick to Hospital. Three have been cast, one died, two destroyed and thirty eight have been returned	
			J W Dawson O/C 12 Mobile Section Capt AVC ? Dawson	

2353 Wt. W2544/1454 700,000 5/15 D. D. & L. A.D.S.S./Forms/C. 2118.

Instructions regarding War Diaries and Intelligence Summaries are contained in F. S. Regs., Part II. and the Staff Manual respectively. Title pages will be prepared in manuscript.

WAR DIARY

or

INTELLIGENCE SUMMARY.

(Erase heading not required.)

Army Form C. 2118.

Place	Date	Hour	Summary of Events and Information	Remarks and references to Appendices

2353 Wt. W2544/1454 700,000 5/15 D. D. & L. A.D.S.S./Forms/C. 2118.

Instructions regarding War Diaries and Intelligence Summaries are contained in F. S. Regs., Part II. and the Staff Manual respectively. Title pages will be prepared in manuscript.

WAR DIARY
or
INTELLIGENCE SUMMARY.
(Erase heading not required.)

Army Form C. 2118.

Vol 19

Place	Date	Hour	Summary of Events and Information	Remarks and references to Appendices
			Confidential	
			War Diary	
			of	
			Captain J. M. Dawson AVC.	
			12 Mobile Section	
			7 Division.	
			From 1st September 1916 to 30th Sept 1916.	

2353 Wt. W2544/1454 700,000 5/15 D. D. & L. A.D.S.S./Forms/C. 2118.

Instructions regarding War Diaries and Intelligence Summaries are contained in F. S. Regs., Part II. and the Staff Manual respectively. Title pages will be prepared in manuscript.

WAR DIARY
or
INTELLIGENCE SUMMARY.
(Erase heading not required.)

Army Form C. 2118.

Place	Date	Hour	Summary of Events and Information	Remarks and references to Appendices
1916	September 1st		Paid a visit to collecting station, Evacuating twenty four sick horses including three animals cast by D D R., sent out float for a horse of 59 R F A. D Battn which had received a bad kick and was unable to walk.	
	"	2	Engaged to-day in ordinary work of Section, at request of O.C of 7th D.A.C have had to send back two 7th D.A.C drivers who were attached to the Section in exchange for which I have had two Gunners sent, I understand the column is in rather need of drivers having had a number of casualties among the latter recently	
	"	3	Ordinary work of Section, Have had a visit from A.D.V.S., Sent for a sick horse of 7th Div Head Quarters	
	"	4	I have to-day sent out for a sick horse which another Mobile declined to admit on the grounds I understand, that it was not of their own Division, Picked out a number of Animals for evacuation	
	"	5	Evacuated fifteen sick horses, Visited advanced collecting Station and sent up float for a horse which they had admitted belonging to 7 D.A.C.	
	"	6	Busy this morning inspecting all cases in the Section and deciding what to evacuate, Received a visit from A.D.V.S., and he had a look at some suspected mange cases, conferring with him as to these cases, Destroyed a horse of 7th D.A.C. admitted with shrapnel wounds in back & side a bad case, Also sent for to visit the sick animals at Rebemont an adjoining village which I did	
	"	7	I have evacuated 26 horses today, Sent out float for a horse of 104 Batt 22 Bde R F A Shrapnel wounds, Visited the A D V S at Rebemont	

2353 Wt. W2544/1454 700,000 5/15 D. D. & L. A.D.S.S./Forms/C. 2118.

Instructions regarding War Diaries and Intelligence Summaries are contained in F. S. Regs., Part II. and the Staff Manual respectively. Title pages will be prepared in manuscript.

WAR DIARY
or
INTELLIGENCE SUMMARY.
(Erase heading not required.)

Army Form C. 2118.

Place	Date	Hour	Summary of Events and Information	Remarks and references to Appendices
	1916 Sept 8th		At request of DDVS. I have sent float for a horse left behind by 35th Div Am Col at Daours beyond CORBIE also to BONNAY for two sick horses left behind by 33 Div Am Col, Mallein tested the following remounts 13 of 7th Signals 2 Royal Warwicks, 2-22 Machine Gun Section 2, 2nd Manchesters, have been instructed to do this by ADVS, these remounts only came up a short time since, but apparently came in a boat with some infected animals	
	" 9th		Picked out a number of horses for evacuation, Understand that the Division is moving back but that the Section will go forward about the 11th as the Artillery is to remain in action for a while, I shall probably go under canvas nr Meaulte on right of Albert, DAQMG warns that 75 remounts for 7th Division arrive MERICOURT Railhead today 12-30. So have been down with necessary men but the animals did not arrive until 5.30 to 6 o'clock, and close on 8 before the horses could be cleared.	
	" 10th		Evacuated 28 sick horses today, Shall move the Section tomorrow Monday morning	
	" 11th		Section moved by road to a camp left of Meaulte, near 7th DAC Waggon lines where the advance party have already took up quarters, find sick horses already admitted that are animals F.13th 14th RHA has died with twist of bowel, I have destroyed 2 animals of 7th DAC with bad Shrapnel wound and which were helpless cases.	
	" 12		Looked over horses & picked out number for early evacuation	
	" 13		I have admitted a large number of horses with debility no less than 14 from 7th DAC & from Brigades of Artillery which I intend to evacuate	
	" 14		Evacuated 52 cases this morning chiefly debility cases, sent float to Morlancourt for sick horse, ADVS	

2353 Wt. W2544/1454 700,000 5/15 D. D. & L. A.D.S.S./Forms/C. 2118.

Instructions regarding War Diaries and Intelligence Summaries are contained in F. S. Regs., Part II. and the Staff Manual respectively. Title pages will be prepared in manuscript.

WAR DIARY
or
INTELLIGENCE SUMMARY.
(Erase heading not required.)

Army Form C. 2118.

Place	Date	Hour	Summary of Events and Information	Remarks and references to Appendices
1916 September	15		who is carrying with the Section instructs me to send out an advance collecting party, I have taken over Vet charge of 7th Bn ... No 1 Coy for the time being	
"	16		The advance party is to be held back for a while, ADVS informs me that a conducting party has been placed with ... at Meaulte for use of Mobile Evacuating from Meaulte Albert or Bécordel or Edgehill, party consists of 2 Sergeants two Corporals and ... men	
"	17		Sent out advance collecting party, picked out 52 horses for evacuation, Sent [illegible] for horse of 1st Batt 22 Bde RFA Shrapnel ..., Destroyed a horse of 12 Batt 35 Bde Shrapnel wound Mouth, a bad case, noted	
"	"	18	Evacuated 52 horses today, destroyed a horse of 13 Batt RFA 15 Bde [illegible] in with a fracture of O.F. Radius, the animal should never have been sent in, but should have been destroyed immediately when much unnecessary suffering would have been avoided to the animal.	
"	"	19	Am informed the DAC to which Collecting Station is attached have been recalled to a place ... this morning, ADVS advises that Collecting Station should now attach themselves to 22nd Bde RFA arranging for this to be done immediately, my Sergeant to report to Lieut ... AVC ...	
"	"	20	arranging to evacuate 2 truck loads of sick horses, made out a return of horses & vehicles for D.A.D.V.S. in case a move by train takes place	
	"	21	Evacuated 13 sick horses today, Ordinary work of Section	
"	"	22	Must evacuate again tomorrow	
"	"	23	Admitted a number of debility cases today, evacuated 24 cases & must evacuate the rest as soon as possible in case the Section should be instructed to move which in all probability will take place soon	
	.	24	Evacuated 82 cases today chiefly debility cases from artillery Bdes, Since the 11th up to 23 inst 228 animals have been received in this Section	

Instructions regarding War Diaries and Intelligence Summaries are contained in F. S. Regs., Part II. and the Staff Manual respectively. Title pages will be prepared in manuscript.

WAR DIARY
or
INTELLIGENCE SUMMARY.
(Erase heading not required.)

Army Form C. 2118.

Place	Date	Hour	Summary of Events and Information	Remarks and references to Appendices
1916.	September	25	Engaged in work of Section, (Hostile aeroplane flew over our lines to-night about 9.30 dropping a few bombs in the vicinity but without damage)	
	"	26	I expect we shall move North in a few days, the Cavalry comes out of action tomorrow, arranging to evacuate sick animals now in Section tomorrow	
	"	27	Evacuated 25 Sick Horses today, The Section will move tomorrow en route for North. Arranging more	
	"	28	More sick animals have turned up, arranged for 16 Mobile (Guards Div) to take these horses & to evacuate them for me, six in number. - Destroyed an animal of 7BW Drum which had a bad fracture of O.H. Tibia - Section moves as far as Bonnay today where we arrive about 5 P.M, admitted more sick horses, which I shall have to evacuate tomorrow.	
	"	29	Arranging to Evacuate eight sick horses from Mericourt Station	
	"	30	Evacuated the eight horses, Section moved to Longueau (Amiens) via Corbie & Cachie, and shall not be entraining until tomorrow morning about 7 AM, ADVS of Division moves with the Section	
			349 Sick animals have been admitted to the Section during the month 334 have been evacuated to Hospital, 7 cast, six have been destroyed and one horse has died and sixteen have been returned cured.	

GM Dawson
Capt AVC
O/C 12 M.V.S.

2353 Wt. W2544/1454 700,000 5/15 D. D. & L. A.D.S.S./Forms/C. 2118.

Army Form C. 2118.

Instructions regarding War Diaries and Intelligence Summaries are contained in F. S. Regs., Part II. and the Staff Manual respectively. Title pages will be prepared in manuscript.

WAR DIARY
or
INTELLIGENCE SUMMARY.
(Erase heading not required.)

Vol 28

Place	Date	Hour	Summary of Events and Information	Remarks and references to Appendices
In the Field.			Confidential War Diary — of — Captain J M. Dawson. A.V.C O/C. 12 Mobile Section 7th Division From 1st October 1916. to 31st October 1916.	

2353 Wt. W2544/1454 700,000 5/15 D. D. & L. A.D.S.S./Forms/C. 2118.

Instructions regarding War Diaries and Intelligence Summaries are contained in F. S. Regs., Part II. and the Staff Manual respectively. Title pages will be prepared in manuscript.

WAR DIARY
or
INTELLIGENCE SUMMARY.
(Erase heading not required.)

Army Form C. 2118.

Place	Date	Hour	Summary of Events and Information	Remarks and references to Appendices
1916	October	1st "	Section entrained at Longeau siding this morning about 8 AM enroute for North, a very monotonous journey but escaped the usual delays. Arrived at HAZEBROUK Station about 6.30, and at Caestre about 7 PM here we detrained and marched to METERAN, were we decided to halt for the night,	
"	"	2nd "	Struck camp at 9.30 this morning, marched to BAILLEUL, here A.D.V.S. left us, his office is to be at this place, Section marched forward to appointed place near NEIPPE, find 31 Mobile Section still in possession 3.30 PM 31 Mobile receive instructions by wire to move at once which they do, arranged with O/C of latter Section to take over his sick horses and to deal with them	
"	"	3rd	Find accommodation here very fair, some very decent horse standings, some of which are covered in, Evacuated eight sick horses arranged to be sent by 31st Mobile, Visited by A.D.V.S. and arranging with him to receive and evacuate a number of debility cases from Divisional Artillery, the following day at 8 AM making necessary preparations.	
"	"	4th	Admitted 130 horses from various Batteries first batch arrived about 5 AM, had little time to take descriptions of these animals, prepare rolls &c and get them to BAILLEUL Station for entraining at 8 AM, however succeeded in doing so together with	

2353 Wt. W2544/1454 700,000 5/15 D. D. & L. A.D.S.S./Forms/C. 2118.

WAR DIARY
or
INTELLIGENCE SUMMARY.
(Erase heading not required.)

Instructions regarding War Diaries and Intelligence Summaries are contained in F. S. Regs., Part II. and the Staff Manual respectively. Title pages will be prepared in manuscript.

Army Form C. 2118.

Place	Date	Hour	Summary of Events and Information	Remarks and references to Appendices
			twenty other sick cases I have in Section, Total evacuated this day is one hundred & fifty	
1916	October	5th	Have taken over veterinary charge of 42 Army Troops RE and 21st Field Ambulance, Paid them both a visit – Horses can only be evacuated from this area on certain days I find arrangements are as follows, Cases fit to walk, sent once a week on Mondays, a four day journey including halts, Bad cases are sent by Barge from BAC ST MAUR on Tuesdays and Thursdays and when necessary by Barge from ESTAIRES on Mondays Horses are divided into three classes A Road cases, B. Barge, C animals fit for retention in Section that is slight cases, A here with the statement is sent each day to ADVS Similar notes have also to be sent on Mondays and Tuesdays with probable number of Barge cases, and on Fridays for Mondays Barge Estaires route if required	
"	"	6th	Engaged in work of Section, Improving horse standings, the place requires a very big cleaning up, whitewashing & the place with little trouble can be made quite satisfactory	
"	"	7th	Have been similarly employed to day, rearranging and cleaning up Section	
"	"	8th	Visited by ADVS to-day and arranging as to disposal of sick horses generally	
		9th	Arranging to evacuate six cases by Barge tomorrow Received 13 debility cases from F Batt 14th RHA – Had to destroy a horse of 7th D.A.Col which had been badly [illegible]	

Instructions regarding War Diaries and Intelligence Summaries are contained in F. S. Regs., Part II. and the Staff Manual respectively. Title pages will be prepared in manuscript.

WAR DIARY
or
INTELLIGENCE SUMMARY.
(Erase heading not required.)

Army Form C. 2118.

Place	Date	Hour	Summary of Events and Information	Remarks and references to Appendices
1916 October	10th		Evacuated six cases today, Received a visit from A.D.V.S	
	" 11th		Visited units under my Veterinary charge, Busy at Station this afternoon.	
	" 12th		Arranging with A.D.V.S. to receive a further number of debility cases from Batteries for evacuation.	
	" 13th		Again saw A.D.V.S. as to evacuation of R.F.A horses which were to be sent in tomorrow making arrangements to receive these cases and to evacuate same by special train from Bailleul Station, Mallened a stray horse which has been brought to station	
	" 14th		Had a very busy day receiving from various Batteries R.F.A 132 debility cases, Have had all my time in to get descriptions and rolls prepared. Special train is to start from Bailleul Station at 10.38 with these cases for 25 Vety Hospital Neufchatel, I have to accompany the train as V.O in charge, two other Mobile are sending a number of animals as well & understand total of load is 280, I provide one NCO and 19 men as conducting party.	
	" 15th		Added nine cases to the 132 making a total evacuated 141, Got horses off in good time this morning, left Bailleul about appointed time but did not arrive at Neufchatel until late and it was dark before animals were unloaded	

2353 Wt. W2544/1454 700,000 5/15 D. D. & L. A.D.S.S./Forms/C. 2118.

Instructions regarding War Diaries and Intelligence Summaries are contained in F. S. Regs., Part II. and the Staff Manual respectively. Title pages will be prepared in manuscript.

WAR DIARY
or
INTELLIGENCE SUMMARY.
(Erase heading not required.)

Army Form C. 2118.

Place	Date	Hour	Summary of Events and Information	Remarks and references to Appendices
1916	Oct	16th	Left for return journey this morning about 2 AM, arrived back at Section about 12 PM. Find wire awaiting me that I have been allotted 15 places for Barge tomorrow; Sent Shot for a horse belonging to 7th Salvage company which I found suffering from Glanders.	
"	"	17th	Arranging to send off 15 Barge cases from Bac St Maur; Issued a number of Remounts which have been sent to the Section for various Units of 7th Division, I have applied to C.R.E for Head covering for horse standings and have received some authority to draw necessary timber, roofing &c for same.	
"	"	18th	Have been allotted 14 places for Thursdays Barge – Visited by A.D.V.S. – Went over to 21 Field Ambulance, saw OC of 3 Section 7 D.A.C. and arranged to receive four debility cases which I intend to include in the 14 horses for evacuation, tomorrow	
"	"	19th	Evacuated 14 horses by Barge this morning – Had to destroy an animal of 14 RHA (formerly Major Webber's charger) and on which I held a Post Mortem examination, I found this animal had Fractured Pelvis.	
"	"	20th	Have received timber from R.E's for head covering for horse standings, and commenced getting the frames together, I have taken over temporary Veterinary charge of 12th and 5th Batteries of 35 R.F.A 42 Army Troops, 11th Labour Batt & 171 Tunnelling Co.	

2353 Wt. W2544/1454 700,000 5/15 D. D. & L. A.D.S.S./Forms/C. 2118.

Army Form C. 2118.

Instructions regarding War Diaries and Intelligence Summaries are contained in F. S. Regs., Part II. and the Staff Manual respectively. Title pages will be prepared in manuscript.

WAR DIARY
or
INTELLIGENCE SUMMARY.
(Erase heading not required.)

Place	Date	Hour	Summary of Events and Information	Remarks and references to Appendices
1916	Oct.	21st	Have been busy at Section to day, improving standings & superintending erection of head-coverings for same	
"	"	22nd	Similarly engaged to-day	
"	"	23rd	Visited 21st Field Ambulance, Sent Horse to Bde HdQrs for Capt Smith's charger	
"	"	24th	Visited by ADVS – Sent Float to 36 D.A.C for horse left there by 7th D.A.C which had received bad lacerated wounds and was unfit to travel. On arrival in Section, I found on examination that this horse was severely cut about and had open joint Off and that I had no alternative but to destroy it at once which I did, tho' very reluctantly as it was quite a good animal, but it was a hopeless case. It appears that this horse one of a team descending a steep hill with a waggon, fell and was dragged some distance along the road by the other horses.	
"	"	25	Busy at Section, This afternoon an explosion occurred at R E Stores near setting fire to buildings, I told off as many men as possible from Section to render assistance. Much damage has been done to outbuildings but main buildings (dwelling house) was saved by strenuous efforts of soldiers present, The buildings were thatched	
"	"	26	Have been allotted 15 places in Barge for tomorrow, Picked out cases but so	

2353 Wt. W2544/1454 700,000 5/15 D. D. & L. A.D.S.S./Forms/C. 2118.

Instructions regarding War Diaries and Intelligence Summaries are contained in F. S. Regs., Part II. and the Staff Manual respectively. Title pages will be prepared in manuscript.

WAR DIARY
or
INTELLIGENCE SUMMARY.

(*Erase heading not required.*)

Army Form C. 2118.

Place	Date	Hour	Summary of Events and Information	Remarks and references to Appendices
			have only ten cases to go, I can retain the remainder	
1916	Oct	27th	Evacuated ten cases by Barge, went in to Bailleul to see ADVS, understand that we shall be shortly moving from present area.	
"	"	28th	Visited by A.D.V.S and arranging as to evacuating ten cases (two mange (Sarcoptic) and eight suspected mange cases) by Road tomorrow Sunday – Inspected feet of men of Section & attached men	
"	"	29th	Evacuated ten skin cases by Road to No 23 Vety Hospital this entails a two days journey each way. Section expects to move from area in a few days – Although we have only been in area a short time numerous cases have been admitted. Visited 23 Fd Amb	
"	"	30	Sent Horse for horse of 58 Batty 35 Bde RFA found in animals at Section that it had open joint and I have had to destroy it. Have been allotted ten places for tomorrow's Barge, picking out cases for evacuation	
"	"	31	Evacuated seven animals by Barge today, Have taken over temporary Vety charge of No 7 and 8 Coys 2nd Remount Park.	
			During the month 423 sick animals have been admitted, 383 sent to Vety Hospitals, 4 have been destroyed Nil died and 30 returned cured, the animals sent up as Remounts have been sent back sick to Hospital being unfit for issue to Units (during the month)	
			J M Dawson Capt A.V.C. 12 Mobile Vety Sectn	

2353 Wt. W2544/1454 700,000 5/15 D. D. & L. A.D.S.S./Forms/C. 2118.

Army Form C. 2118.

Instructions regarding War Diaries and Intelligence Summaries are contained in F. S. Regs., Part II. and the Staff Manual respectively. Title pages will be prepared in manuscript.

WAR DIARY
or
INTELLIGENCE SUMMARY.
(*Erase heading not required.*)

Place	Date	Hour	Summary of Events and Information	Remarks and references to Appendices

2353 Wt. W2544/1454 700,000 5/15 D. D. & L. A.D.S.S./Forms/C. 2118.

Instructions regarding War Diaries and Intelligence Summaries are contained in F. S. Regs., Part II. and the Staff Manual respectively. Title pages will be prepared in manuscript.

WAR DIARY
or
INTELLIGENCE SUMMARY.
(*Erase heading not required.*)

Army Form C. 2118.

Vol 21

Place	Date	Hour	Summary of Events and Information	Remarks and references to Appendices
			Confidential	
			War Diary	
			of	
			Captain J. M. Dawson A.V.C.	
			O/C. 12 Mobile Vety Section 7th Division.	
			From 1st Nov 1916 to 30th Nov 1916.	

2353 Wt. W2544/1454 700,000 5/15 D. D. & L. A.D.S.S./Forms/C. 2118.

Army Form C. 2118.

Instructions regarding War Diaries and Intelligence Summaries are contained in F. S. Regs., Part II. and the Staff Manual respectively. Title pages will be prepared in manuscript.

WAR DIARY
or
INTELLIGENCE SUMMARY.
(Erase heading not required.)

Place	Date	Hour	Summary of Events and Information	Remarks and references to Appendices
1916 Nov	1st		Visited by A.D.V.S. O.C. of 37 Mobile Section 25 Division who is taking over our present Billet on our moving also visited me, supplied him with full information respecting evacuation of sick horses from this area, writing out some notes for his use	
"	2nd		Sent float for horse of 22 Manchesters and to 25th R.F.A., making preparations for move	
"	3rd		Left NIEPPE at 10.30 AM for Meteran, took long route to avoid incoming troops. On arrival at allotted Billet found it occupied by another unit so had to go off in search of fresh quarters for the Section, found a farm where I could put up Section for night at least, Subsequently A.D.V.S called and we went in search of a more suitable place, found farm where 37 Mobile had just lately occupied a very poor place but better than present farm, so arranged to move in morning	
"	4th		Moved off at 7 AM this morning to farm near FLETRE, found my Billet in occupation of Sanitary Section, arranged that they should move out during the day, Subsequently I was able to take possession, O/C Sanitary Sect. dined with me	
"	5th		Busy in Section clearing up & improving horse standings, & getting things in order	

Instructions regarding War Diaries and Intelligence Summaries are contained in F. S. Regs., Part II. and the Staff Manual respectively. Title pages will be prepared in manuscript.

WAR DIARY
or
INTELLIGENCE SUMMARY.
(Erase heading not required.)

Army Form C. 2118.

Place	Date	Hour	Summary of Events and Information	Remarks and references to Appendices
1916 Nov	6th		Visited Units under my charge, Arranging to evacuate two Barge cases tomorrow	
"	7th		Evacuated two Sick cases by Barge. Visited ADVS at his request, and find we have	
"	8th		to move with the Division tomorrow 9th. Sent in six cases to 4th MVS as I am unable to take these with me. Sent the other six cases arriving in Section lines to 37th M.V.S.	
"	9th		Section moved off at 10 AM linking up with Division and marching via HAZEBROUCK to small village of Sercus (SERCUS) arriving about 4. PM, halted here for night. Was able to secure covered standing for most of Section horses	
"	10th		Left Sercus 10AM marched to ST OMER arriving about 2.30 PM. Find I have to Billet Section here instead of St MARTIN as previously instructed, Have no cover for horses but am able to put my men in the French Barracks for the night, Evacuated four ~~sick~~ cast horses to No 23 Vety Hospital which I had brought along with me from FLETRE and cast by DDR	
"	11		Section moved off about 9.30. Have received duplicate order and have had to inquire which of these I have to act on, Subsequently joined up with 21 Field Ambulance and 3 Coy Div Train, arrangements being altered I have	

2353 Wt. W2544/1454 700,000 5/15 D. D. & L. A.D.S.S./Forms/C. 2118.

Instructions regarding War Diaries and Intelligence Summaries are contained in F. S. Regs., Part II. and the Staff Manual respectively. Title pages will be prepared in manuscript.

WAR DIARY
or
INTELLIGENCE SUMMARY.
(Erase heading not required.)

Army Form C. 2118.

Place	Date	Hour	Summary of Events and Information	Remarks and references to Appendices
1916	Nov		to find Billets in or near SERQUES where I arrive about 12-30, Have no accommodation for horses except in open field and very poor Billets for men	
"	"12th		Visited Units under my charge this morning, Saw ADVS this evening	
"	"13th		Arranging to evacuate seven sick horses which have been sent into section, Also visited by ADVS	
"	14th		Evacuated seven sick horses to No 23 Vet Hospital, Section continues to march to morrow	
"	15th		Section moved to HALLINES, Have fairly good Billets for horses & men	
"	16th		Section continued march as far as GREUPPE (BOMY) Have to put up horses in field with 3 Co of Train	
"	17th		Division is to rest to-day. Left a sick horse of 3rd Co of Train with an Inhabitant. Received 40 Remounts for distribution, these I had to fetch from some distance. Visited by ADVS and was instructed to issue 22 of these Remounts as per his list which he gave me. Subsequently issuing same	
"	18th		Left Bomy for EPS Have had good weather for move so far but today it is very cold with slight fall of snow, turning to bitter wind with sleet	

Instructions regarding War Diaries and Intelligence Summaries are contained in F. S. Regs., Part II. and the Staff Manual respectively. Title pages will be prepared in manuscript.

WAR DIARY
or
INTELLIGENCE SUMMARY.
(Erase heading not required.)

Army Form C. 2118.

Place	Date	Hour	Summary of Events and Information	Remarks and references to Appendices
1916 Dec			Find accommodation at Cps very poor	
"	19th		Left Ch and marched to HAUTECOTE, horses and men have to be scattered in different parts of village – a very tedious march	
"	20th		Moved from Hautecote to BEAUVOIR WAVANS, stayed the night	
"	21st		Continued march to day as far as BEAUVAL remained the night	
"	22nd		Left Beauval and marched on to ACHEUX where arrived about 3.30 Camped in field on edge of wood near railway between Acheux & FORCEVILLE	
"	23rd		Remained at Acheux to-day	
"	24th		Visited by ADVS, am instructed to move Section to BERTRANCOURT On arrival at latter place find 42nd Mobile Section in Billets but under order to move tomorrow	
"	25th		42nd MVS moved off this morning leaving nine sick cases with me, on examination of these animals find 4 are in such a bad state that I have no alternative but to shoot them which I have done	
"	26th		Evacuated 19 sick cases today. Visited by ADVS.	
"	27th		Evacuated 24 sick horses today, at present have only received 5 cases from my own Division the remainder are from other Divisions than 9th.	

Instructions regarding War Diaries and Intelligence Summaries are contained in F. S. Regs., Part II. and the Staff Manual respectively. Title pages will be prepared in manuscript.

WAR DIARY
or
INTELLIGENCE SUMMARY.
(Erase heading not required.)

Army Form C. 2118.

Place	Date	Hour	Summary of Events and Information	Remarks and references to Appendices
1916 Nov	28th		Evacuated 24 sick horses, sent float for horse belonging to 21 Field ambulance.	
	29th		Evacuated 31 sick horses today. Standings for horses are very bad here, if possible must get some bricks and chalk & try in some way to improve present state of affairs	
"	30th		Sent float for mule of 91 Machine Gun Co. Partial Radial Paralysis. Also to 41 RFA Wagon lines for horse wound punctured foot. Since arriving in this area a week ago I have admitted to Section 111 sick cases and evacuated 98 cases to hospital. Out of the number admitted 14 only belong to this Division, all the others were from other Divisions in the neighbourhood.	
			During the month 147 horses have been admitted 132 evacuated to Vet. Hospital 4 have been destroyed and four returned as cured. The greater part of the month the Section was on the march	
			G. W. Dawson Capt AVC O/C 12 Mobile Vet Sec 9th Div. 1/12/16	

2353 Wt. W2544/1454 700,000 5/15 D. D. & L. A.D.S.S./Forms/C. 2118.

Army Form C. 2118.

Instructions regarding War Diaries and Intelligence Summaries are contained in F. S. Regs., Part II. and the Staff Manual respectively. Title pages will be prepared in manuscript.

WAR DIARY
or
INTELLIGENCE SUMMARY.

(Erase heading not required.)

Place	Date	Hour	Summary of Events and Information	Remarks and references to Appendices

2353 Wt. W2544/1454 700,000 5/15 D. D. & L. A.D.S.S./Forms/C. 2118.

Army Form C. 2118.

Instructions regarding War Diaries and Intelligence Summaries are contained in F. S. Regs., Part II. and the Staff Manual respectively. Title pages will be prepared in manuscript.

WAR DIARY
or
INTELLIGENCE SUMMARY.
(Erase heading not required.)

Vol 22

Place	Date	Hour	Summary of Events and Information	Remarks and references to Appendices

Confidential

War Diary

of

Captain J. M. Dawson A.V.C.

12. Mobile Vety Section.
7th Division.

From 1st to 31st Dec 1916.

2353 Wt. W2544/1454 700,000 5/15 D. D. & L. A.D.S.S./Forms/C. 2118.

Instructions regarding War Diaries and Intelligence Summaries are contained in F. S. Regs., Part II. and the Staff Manual respectively. Title pages will be prepared in manuscript.

WAR DIARY
or
INTELLIGENCE SUMMARY.
(Erase heading not required.)

Army Form C. 2118.

Place	Date	Hour	Summary of Events and Information	Remarks and references to Appendices
1916 December	1st		Evacuated eight sick horses today, visited units under my charge	
"	" 2nd		Evacuated sixteen sick horses, visited by A.D.V.S. arranging to evacuate again tomorrow	
"	" 3rd		Evacuated twenty one sick horses, destroyed a horse belonging 161 R.F.A. (over reach NF)	
"	" 4th		Evacuated sixteen sick horses today and destroyed one of 168 Bde RFA 33 DW - Gunshot O Stark	
"	" 5th		Destroyed a horse of 21st Field Ambulance, visiting units under my charge	
"	" 6th		Evacuated eight sick horses, visited by ADVS.	
"	" 9th		Visited units under my charge, which includes 22 Inf Bde 3 Co of Train 23rd Field Ambulance and four other units	
"	" 10th		Engaged in work of Section and visiting units	
"	" 11th		The like, visited by A.D.V.S.	
"	" 12th		Evacuated sick horses (six) today also two horses cast by D.D.R.	
"	" 13th		Busy in Section and visiting units under my charge	
"	" 14th		Am doing duty of ADVS in absence of Major Glasse who is on leave	
"	" 15th		Evacuated twelve sick horses to day, busy visiting units, ADVS office	
"	" 16th		ADVS office, Section and units	

2353 Wt. W2544/1454 700,000 5/15 D. D. & L. A.D.S.S./Forms/C. 2118.

Instructions regarding War Diaries and Intelligence Summaries are contained in F. S. Regs., Part II. and the Staff Manual respectively. Title pages will be prepared in manuscript.

WAR DIARY
or
INTELLIGENCE SUMMARY.
(Erase heading not required.)

Army Form C. 2118.

Place	Date	Hour	Summary of Events and Information	Remarks and references to Appendices
1916	December	17th	Visiting Units, A D V S office.	
	"	18th	Arranging with 11th Mobile Section to evacuate 2 suspected mange cases tomorrow	
	"	19th	Evacuated nineteen sick cases, collected horse left behind by 168. R.F.A. D Batt'y	
	"	20th	Visiting units under my charge, attending A D V S office	
	"	21st	Similarly engaged to day	
	"	22nd	At A D V S office relative to weekly returns from V.O.s of Division	
	"	23rd	Evacuated seven sick horses, visited Units under my charge, also those under Capt Evans the latter officer being indisposed	
	"	24th	Similarly engaged to day, Busy at Section	
	"	25th	Xmas day, Only necessary work has been done in the Section, in accordance with wishes expressed by Corps Commander that work should cease as far as possible on this day	
	"	26th	Busy visiting Units under my charge and with work of Section, at A D V S office	
	"	27th	Evacuated eight sick horses to day, Three horses were injured in the Village to day by Bomb from Hostile Air craft Attending to these animals with Capt R B Crute of 22 Infy Bde, 1 animal belonged to 7th Pontoon Park and two to 2 Siege Co R A R E's	
	"	28	A D V S returned to day = I start leave tomorrow	

Army Form C. 2118.

Instructions regarding War Diaries and Intelligence Summaries are contained in F. S. Regs., Part II. and the Staff Manual respectively. Title pages will be prepared in manuscript.

WAR DIARY
or
INTELLIGENCE SUMMARY.
(Erase heading not required.)

Place	Date	Hour	Summary of Events and Information	Remarks and references to Appendices
	1918 Dec	29th	Went on leave	
	"	30th	On leave.	
	"	31st	On leave, During the month ending today 168 Sick horses have been admitted to the Section, 147 have been evacuated to Hospital, 5 have been returned as cured and five had to be destroyed	

[illegible signature]
for Capt. J. M. [illegible]
O/C 12 Mobile Section
AVC

2353 Wt. W2544/1454 700,000 5/15 D. D. & L. A.D.S.S./Forms/C. 2118.

Army Form C. 2118.

Instructions regarding War Diaries and Intelligence Summaries are contained in F. S. Regs., Part II. and the Staff Manual respectively. Title pages will be prepared in manuscript.

WAR DIARY
or
INTELLIGENCE SUMMARY.

(Erase heading not required.)

Place	Date	Hour	Summary of Events and Information	Remarks and references to Appendices

2353 Wt. W2544/1454 700,000 5/15 D. D. & L. A.D.S.S./Forms/C. 2118.

Instructions regarding War Diaries and Intelligence Summaries are contained in F. S. Regs., Part II. and the Staff Manual respectively. Title pages will be prepared in manuscript.

WAR DIARY
or
INTELLIGENCE SUMMARY.
(Erase heading not required.)

Army Form C. 2118.

Mob Vety Sec
Vol 23

Place	Date	Hour	Summary of Events and Information	Remarks and references to Appendices
			Confidential	
			War Diary	
			of	
			Captain J M Dawson A.V.C	
			O/C 12 Mobile Section A.V.C. 7th Division.	
			From 1st January 1917 to 31st January 1917	

2353 Wt. W2544/1454 700,000 5/15 D. D. & L. A.D.S.S./Forms/C. 2118.

Instructions regarding War Diaries and Intelligence Summaries are contained in F. S. Regs., Part II. and the Staff Manual respectively. Title pages will be prepared in manuscript.

WAR DIARY
or
INTELLIGENCE SUMMARY.
(Erase heading not required.)

Army Form C. 2118.

Place	Date	Hour	Summary of Events and Information	Remarks and references to Appendices
1917	Jan 1st	to 8th:	On leave	
	"	9	Bertrancourt (Somme) Evacuated 32 sick horses today.	
	"	10	At Section, visited by A D V S. — arranging to again evacuate tomorrow	
	"	11	Evacuated 22 sick horses to day, Busy at Section	
	"	12	At Section most of day, visited units under my charge	
	"	13	Destroyed three horses, one from 35th RFA HQ. Broken Knees, one from 10th Batt and one from 106 Batt 22 R.F.A. had debility cases — at Section	
	"	14	Evacuated 65 sick cases to day, Destroyed horse of 4 Sec 7 D.A.C. Dermatitis necrotic and two horses the 7 DAC 2 Section Catarrh case and one from same unit debility died	
	"	15	Destroyed ~~seven~~ horses one 107 Batt 22 RFA debility and 3 [illegible] 2 Section 2 debility and one dermatitis necrotic, two 106 Batt 22 RFA with debility and one of South Wales Borders a bad sick case	
	"	16	Evacuated 33 sick horses to day, — visited units under my charge	
	"	17	Destroyed 3 horses 105 Batt 22 RFA with debility — at Section.	
	"	18	Visited units under my charge, Evacuated 58 horses ~~under my charge~~	

2353 Wt. W2544/1454 700,000 5/15 D. D. & L. A.D.S.S./Forms/C. 2118.

Instructions regarding War Diaries and Intelligence Summaries are contained in F. S. Regs., Part II. and the Staff Manual respectively. Title pages will be prepared in manuscript.

WAR DIARY
or
INTELLIGENCE SUMMARY.
(Erase heading not required.)

Army Form C. 2118.

Place	Date	Hour	Summary of Events and Information	Remarks and references to Appendices
1917 Jan			Destroyed three debility cases received from 105 Batt 22 RFA	
"	19		Evacuated twenty nine cases to-day, visited units under my charge. Understand Division goes out of action and moves to rest area in coming week, Later received wire that Mobile will remain in present area with artillery moves	
"	20		Destroyed a bad debility case received from 2 Sec 75 DAC, visited units	
"	21		Destroyed four horses of 106 Bty 22 RFA. three debility cases & one dermatitis necrotic also a debility case from 104 Batt — Evacuated 38 sick cases	
"	22		today the 22nd (not 21st) — visiting units	
"	23		Visiting units, and engaged in Section	
"	24		Evacuated 52 sick horses today, destroyed one of No 2 Sec 78 DAC. Dermatitis necrotic and one of 104 Bty 22 RFA. debility	
"	25		Visited units under my charge, these are some distance from this place and most difficult to get at	
	26		Have received orders to join the Division at Marieux (about 8 kilometres from here) tomorrow and that 42 Mobile 32 Division will relieve me	

2353 Wt. W2544/1454 700,000 5/15 D. D. & L. A.D.S.S./Forms/C. 2118.

Instructions regarding War Diaries and Intelligence Summaries are contained in F. S. Regs., Part II. and the Staff Manual respectively. Title pages will be prepared in manuscript.

WAR DIARY
or
INTELLIGENCE SUMMARY.
(Erase heading not required.)

Army Form C. 2118.

Place	Date	Hour	Summary of Events and Information	Remarks and references to Appendices
	1917 Jan 26		Evacuated seven sick cases. Destroyed two horses ? D A C, one Addison's and the other dermatitis necrotic, I have to arrange for 1 NCO & 4 men to be left behind with relieving Mobile — visited by A D V S — our artillery will send sick horses to 12 Mobile	
	27		Moved Section to Warlieux, left behind 43 sick cases (with labels & descriptive rolls) which were admitted a few hours before moving off, Arrived Warlieux about 12-30, there is not sufficient standings for horses, the men have huts. A most bleak place for sick horses, so exposed.	
	" 28		I believe we move from this place about Tuesday — No horses admitted	
	" 29		At Section, Collected 1 horse and 1 mule from Ranchicourt 5th Army H Q Mange & Stray.	
	" 30		At Section, Understand Section does not move for a few days.	
	" 31		At Section, The number of animals dealt with this month has been much heavier than any previous month (so far as I can find out) since the Section arrived in France. During month 514 cases have been admitted 482 transferred to Hospital 13 have been cured 33 destroyed and 4 died.	

J W Dawson
Capt A V C
O/C 12 Mobile Section

2353 Wt. W2544/1454 700,000 5/15 D. D. & L. A.D.S.S./Forms/C. 2118.

Instructions regarding War Diaries and Intelligence Summaries are contained in F. S. Regs., Part II. and the Staff Manual respectively. Title pages will be prepared in manuscript.

WAR DIARY

or

INTELLIGENCE SUMMARY.

(Erase heading not required.)

Army Form C. 2118.

Place	Date	Hour	Summary of Events and Information	Remarks and references to Appendices

2353 Wt. W2544/1454 700,000 5/15 D. D. & L. A.D.S.S./Forms/C. 2118.

Army Form C. 2118.

Vol 24

Instructions regarding War Diaries and Intelligence Summaries are contained in F. S. Regs., Part II. and the Staff Manual respectively. Title pages will be prepared in manuscript.

WAR DIARY
or
INTELLIGENCE SUMMARY.
(*Erase heading not required.*)

Place	Date	Hour	Summary of Events and Information	Remarks and references to Appendices
			Confidential	
			WAR DIARY	
			— of —	
			Captain J.M. Dawson A.V.C.	
			12. Mobile Vety Section.	
			7th Division.	
			From 1st February 1917 to 28th February 1917.	

2353 Wt. W2544/1454 700,000 5/15 D. D. & L. A.D.S.S./Forms/C. 2118.

Instructions regarding War Diaries and Intelligence Summaries are contained in F. S. Regs., Part II. and the Staff Manual respectively. Title pages will be prepared in manuscript.

WAR DIARY
or
INTELLIGENCE SUMMARY.
(Erase heading not required.)

Army Form C. 2118.

Place	Date	Hour	Summary of Events and Information	Remarks and references to Appendices
1918	February	1st	At Section — Visited Units under my charge.	
	"	2nd	Visited by DDVS and ADVS and arranging as to Evacuation of Horses from this area, I have to share 8 trucks every Monday Wednesday and Friday with 19th Division	
	"	3rd	At Section	
	"	4th	At Section	
	"	5th	At Section	
	"	6	Destroyed horse of 91 Inf Bde 1 Staffords Shrapnel hip & back	
	"	7	At Section seeing to improvement of standings and completing head cover of same	
	"	8	At Section	
	"	9	At Section	
	"	10	Destroyed a bad fractured hip mule case received from 5th RE, visited Units	
	"	11	At Section and Units, arranging to evacuate tomorrow.	
	"	12	Evacuated 8 sick cases today, destroyed horse of 25 RGA [illegible] also one from [illegible]	
	"	13	At Section and Units arranging to evacuate a number of Mange cases tomorrow	
	"	14	Evacuated 63 cases of suspected mange, cases chiefly from 46 Reserve Park and 111 RGA.	

2353 Wt. W2544/1454 700,000 5/15 D. D. & L. A.D.S.S./Forms/C. 2118.

Instructions regarding War Diaries and Intelligence Summaries are contained in F. S. Regs., Part II. and the Staff Manual respectively. Title pages will be prepared in manuscript.

WAR DIARY
or
INTELLIGENCE SUMMARY.
(Erase heading not required.)

Army Form C. 2118.

Place	Date	Hour	Summary of Events and Information	Remarks and references to Appendices
			Destroyed a case of fracture leg of 46 Reserve Park	
1917 February	15		At Section and visiting units	
"	16		Evacuated 24 Sick cases today. Destroyed three horses of 1 Sec 7th D.A.C. One of 60 RFA 15 Division, and one 106 13th RFA.	
"	17		Destroyed a horse of 2 Section 7 D.A.C. debility, at Section	
"	18		Arranging to evacuate six train of sick class tomorrow, including 11 cart horses of 3rd Corps Car cart by D.D.R., Sent Sgt. to Station for sick horses, destroyed horse received from 61 details RHA [illegible]	
"	19		Evacuated 38 sick cases and 11 cart horses, Sent Sgt. to 22 Corps Bn for sick horse	
"	20		Understand Division moves to forward area in a few days, probably Thursday, arranging to evacuate 8 trucks of horses tomorrow, destroyed two very bad debility cases received from 22 RFA 104 Bde and one case [illegible], from 14 RHA BAC.	
"	21		Evacuated 8 trucks horses today, Received orders to move to Bertrancourt tomorrow	
"	22		Moved to Bertrancourt took over former standings and billets, hot day and road in bad condition thro' heavy traffic	
"	23		Busy at Section, visited by A.D.V.S. making out weekly returns	
"	24		Morning - at Section, afternoon, visiting units, arranging with A.D.V.S. as to evacuation of horses	

2353 Wt. W2544/1454 700,000 5/15 D. D. & L. A.D.S.S./Forms/C. 2118.

Instructions regarding War Diaries and Intelligence Summaries are contained in F. S. Regs., Part II. and the Staff Manual respectively. Title pages will be prepared in manuscript.

WAR DIARY
or
INTELLIGENCE SUMMARY.
(Erase heading not required.)

Army Form C. 2118.

Place	Date	Hour	Summary of Events and Information	Remarks and references to Appendices
1917 February	24th		in future, and found I had to share 16 trucks Monday Wednesdays and Fridays with three other Mobile Sections Loading at Beaussart Railhead. ADVS to arrange same	
"	25th		Arranging to evacuate 21 sick cases tomorrow, visited by ADVS, destroyed horse of A58 RFA 11 Division	
"	26		Evacuated 21 sick horses. Visiting units under my charge	
"	27		Arranging to evacuate three trucks of horses tomorrow. Visited by ADVS	
"	28		Evacuated sick cases today, sent [illegible] to [illegible] for horse of MMP	
			Number of sick cases admitted during the month totalled 250. 227 were transferred to Base Hospital 17 were destroyed 1 died and 8 were returned cured	
			[illegible signature] Capt AVC O/C 12 Mobile Section [illegible]	

2353 Wt. W2544/1454 700,000 5/15 D. D. & L. A.D.S.S./Forms/C. 2118.

Instructions regarding War Diaries and Intelligence Summaries are contained in F. S. Regs., Part II. and the Staff Manual respectively. Title pages will be prepared in manuscript.

WAR DIARY
or
INTELLIGENCE SUMMARY.
(Erase heading not required.)

Army Form C. 2118.

Place	Date	Hour	Summary of Events and Information	Remarks and references to Appendices

2353 Wt. W2544/1454 700,000 5/15 D. D. & L. A.D.S.S./Forms/C. 2118.

Instructions regarding War Diaries and Intelligence Summaries are contained in F. S. Regs., Part II. and the Staff Manual respectively. Title pages will be prepared in manuscript.

WAR DIARY
or
INTELLIGENCE SUMMARY.
(Erase heading not required.)

Army Form C. 2118.

Vol 25

Place	Date	Hour	Summary of Events and Information	Remarks and references to Appendices
			Confidential.	
			War Diary of Captain J. M. Dawson A.V.C.	
			O/c 12 Mobile Section 7th Division.	
			1st March 1917 to 31st March 1917.	

2353 Wt. W2544/1454 700,000 5/15 D. D. & L. A.D.S.S./Forms/C. 2118.

Instructions regarding War Diaries and Intelligence Summaries are contained in F. S. Regs., Part II. and the Staff Manual respectively. Title pages will be prepared in manuscript.

WAR DIARY
or
INTELLIGENCE SUMMARY.
(Erase heading not required.)

Army Form C. 2118.

Place	Date	Hour	Summary of Events and Information	Remarks and references to Appendices
1917	March	1st	Arranging to evacuate thirty five sick cases tomorrow, Examining and arranging what cases to send	
"		2nd	Evacuated thirty eight cases, visiting units under my charge, completing weekly returns. Destroyed three horses 1-312 RFA. Wounds lacerated 1-14 RHA O.H.Q. a ball kick N Rock and one 311 RFA. Debility & Exhaustion	
"		3rd	Visited units, at Station	
"		4th	Arranging to evacuate two trucks of sick horses tomorrow, Picking out cases	
"		5th	Evacuated 12 sick cases, also one horse cast by DDR for vice. Visited by ADVS.	
"		6th	At Station, Visited units	
"		7th	Similarly engaged to day. Have veterinary charge of several units and find time fully occupied, some units being very difficult to get at being in out of way places and roads bad	
"		8th	Destroyed horse of 16 Sy Batt RGA. suffering from exhaustion, Sent Stone for horse of 15 Reserve Park on instructions of DDVS.	
"		9th	Evacuated fourteen sick cases today Destroyed horse of 31 Division with Exhaustion	

2353 Wt. W2544/1454 700,000 5/15 D. D. & L. A.D.S.S./Forms/C. 2118.

Instructions regarding War Diaries and Intelligence Summaries are contained in F. S. Regs., Part II. and the Staff Manual respectively. Title pages will be prepared in manuscript.

WAR DIARY
or
INTELLIGENCE SUMMARY.
(Erase heading not required.)

Army Form C. 2118.

Place	Date	Hour	Summary of Events and Information	Remarks and references to Appendices
1917 March	10th,		Visited units, admitted 11 sick horses for evacuation from 31 Mobile Section 19 Division, which were moving from area today. Visited by ADVS	
"	11th		Arranging for evacuation of twenty five cases tomorrow, also cases left by 31st Mobile Section yesterday, Sent float for horse of 155 AFA. Destroyed horse of 54 RE	
"	12th		Evacuated 37 cases to-day, Visited units. Destroyed horse of 155 AFA Debility	
"	13th		Visited by A.D.V.S. – at Section. Destroyed horse of 59 FAB. Punctured sole NH	
"	14th		Evacuated fourteen sick cases today.	
"	15th		Visited units – arranging to evacuate sick horses tomorrow	
"	16th		Evacuated eleven horses today, Visited units	
"	17th		Visited by A.D.V.S. Am warned that Section will finally move in a few days	
"	18th		Went with ADVS to Mailley Maillet with a view to finding billets and standings, H.6 has moved today, Regret DDVS called whilst I was absent Destroyed two horses one of 35 RFA. Debility also one of 58 RFA. Debility	
"	19th		Evacuated 45 cases today, Sent advance part on to take over horse standings &c at Mailley Destroyed horse of 35 RFA, 11 Division Gunshot case also one of A/86 RFA Debility	

Instructions regarding War Diaries and Intelligence Summaries are contained in F. S. Regs., Part II. and the Staff Manual respectively. Title pages will be prepared in manuscript.

WAR DIARY
or
INTELLIGENCE SUMMARY.
(Erase heading not required.)

Army Form C. 2118.

Place	Date	Hour	Summary of Events and Information	Remarks and references to Appendices
1917	March 20th		Section moved to Mailley Maillet	
"	21st		Evacuated six horses today Destroyed horse of 35 RFA. Wounded sc	
"	22nd		Arranging to again evacuate tomorrow, Visited units under my charge	
"	23rd		Evacuated 38 sick cases today – at Section	
"	24th		Visited units and engaged at Section, arranging with ADVS to obtain services of motor ambulance to take sick cases which were unable to walk to station tomorrow	
"	25th		As a number of cases have been admitted find I must evacuate six truck loads tomorrow, am unable to obtain help of motor ambulance	
"	26th		Evacuated forty four sick cases today, motor float was available after all and arrived in good time taking six float cases to Railhead, a great help, Destroyed a horse of 58 RFA 11 DW	
"	27th		Arranging to evacuate five trucks of horses tomorrow, Engaged at Section today	
"	28th		Evacuated three ulcerative cellulitis cases and 29 ordinary cases today, On instructions of DDVS went to collect two sick horses of 48 Div Train at Beaussart, find they were collected same day as left reported this to A.D.V.S.	

2353 Wt. W2544/1454 700,000 5/15 D. D. & L. A.D.S.S./Forms/C. 2118.

Instructions regarding War Diaries and Intelligence Summaries are contained in F. S. Regs., Part II. and the Staff Manual respectively. Title pages will be prepared in manuscript.

WAR DIARY
or
INTELLIGENCE SUMMARY.
(*Erase heading not required.*)

Army Form C. 2118.

Place	Date	Hour	Summary of Events and Information	Remarks and references to Appendices
1917 March	29th		Arranging to evacuate five trucks of Sick Horses tomorrow, have admitted a Number of Sick Horses from various Heavy Batts during the time I have been in this town, — at Section	
"	30th		Evacuated to Hospital forty sick Horses, Visited ADVS at his office at Courcelles and conferring generally with him, Away most of day	
"	31		Visited Units under my charge — at Section.	
			During the month 387 sick horses have been admitted 322 have been transferred to Hospital 12 have been returned cured, 3 have died (all three Pneumonia cases) and 14 have been destroyed. Out of a total of 387 horses admitted this month only 107 came from the 9th Division.	

1st April 1917.

J H Dawson
Capt AVC O/c
12 Mobile Section
9th Division

2353 Wt. W2544/1454 700,000 5/15 D. D. & L. A.D.S.S./Forms/C. 2118.

Army Form C. 2118.

Instructions regarding War Diaries and Intelligence Summaries are contained in F. S. Regs., Part II. and the Staff Manual respectively. Title pages will be prepared in manuscript.

WAR DIARY
or
INTELLIGENCE SUMMARY.

(Erase heading not required.)

Place	Date	Hour	Summary of Events and Information	Remarks and references to Appendices

2353 Wt. W2544/1454 700,000 5/15 D. D. & L. A.D.S.S./Forms/C. 2118.

Instructions regarding War Diaries and Intelligence Summaries are contained in F. S. Regs., Part II. and the Staff Manual respectively. Title pages will be prepared in manuscript.

WAR DIARY
or
INTELLIGENCE SUMMARY.
(Erase heading not required.)

Army Form C. 2118.

Mob Vety Sec

Vol 26

Place	Date	Hour	Summary of Events and Information	Remarks and references to Appendices
			Confidential.	

War Diary
— of —
Captain J. M. Dawson A.V.C.

12 Mobile Veterinary Section
7th Division.

From 1st April to 30th April 1917.

2353 Wt. W2544/1454 700,000 5/15 D. D. & L. A.D.S.S./Forms/C. 2118.

Instructions regarding War Diaries and Intelligence Summaries are contained in F. S. Regs., Part II. and the Staff Manual respectively. Title pages will be prepared in manuscript.

WAR DIARY
or
INTELLIGENCE SUMMARY.
(Erase heading not required.)

Army Form C. 2118.

Place	Date	Hour	Summary of Events and Information	Remarks and references to Appendices
	1st April 1917		Arranging to evacuate four truck loads of sick horses to morrow, Destroyed a horse of 5th Siege Batty with PWN and debility, Received wire to move to Courcelles tomorrow, Sent on advance party to Courcelles as instructed by A.D.V.S Evacuated 25 sick horses today	
"	"	2	Moved to COURCELLES this morning, Road in bad condition all way, Find camp allotted to me on Courcelles – Achiet-le-Grand Road, Destroyed 4 sick horses today	
"	"	3	Engaged all day at Section	
"	"	4	Arranging to put down brick standings for horses there being plenty of old bricks in the village near, and the ground is very soft here, Had wagon carting bricks for the purpose, it is impossible to allow sick horses to stand for perhaps 3 or 4 days over fetlocks in mud. Destroyed two horses past recovery	
"	"	5	At Section — Visiting Units under my charge	
"	"	6	Similarly engaged today — visited by A.D.V.S.	
"	"	7	Destroyed a case of debility and weakness 4 debility cases have died during the night from exhaustion — weather bitterly cold.	

2353 Wt. W2544/1454 700,000 5/15 D. D. & L. A.D.S.S./Forms/C. 2118.

Instructions regarding War Diaries and Intelligence Summaries are contained in F. S. Regs., Part II. and the Staff Manual respectively. Title pages will be prepared in manuscript.

WAR DIARY
or
INTELLIGENCE SUMMARY.
(Erase heading not required.)

Army Form C. 2118.

Place	Date	Hour	Summary of Events and Information	Remarks and references to Appendices
1917	April	8	Destroyed a case of debility, DDVS advises that I can evacuate sick horses from Achiet le Grand, Bapaume, Ervillers and Ficheux, making own arrangements with RTO previous day	
	"	9	Arranging to evacuate eight truck load of horses tomorrow. Destroyed [illegible] debility eleven horses today. These animals become so weak from debility that once they get down they have no strength to rise again, all efforts to get them on their legs are unavailable, this continually occurs, it is deplorable to see these horses	
	"	10	Evacuated 58 sick cases today, Destroyed a debility case and one died during the night.	
	"	11	Engaged at Section and in office most of day	
	"	12	Find that I am unable to evacuate horses tomorrow no truck being obtainable. This is regrettable as I have a number of horses in and the sooner they ~~[illegible]~~ ~~[illegible]~~ got away from this place the more prospects there are of ~~[illegible]~~ saving [illegible]	are
	"	13	At Section, visited Units under my charge	
	"	14	A number of debility cases have died during the night, the horses are in such poor condition they are unable to stand the severe cold winds snow & sleet we are	

2353 Wt. W2544/1454 700,000 5/15 D. D. & L. A.D.S.S./Forms/C. 2118.

Instructions regarding War Diaries and Intelligence Summaries are contained in F. S. Regs., Part II. and the Staff Manual respectively. Title pages will be prepared in manuscript.

WAR DIARY
or
INTELLIGENCE SUMMARY.
(Erase heading not required.)

Army Form C. 2118.

Place	Date	Hour	Summary of Events and Information	Remarks and references to Appendices
			experiencing [illegible] now.	
1917	Apl	15	Arranging to evacuate 12 truck load of sick horses on 17th. At [illegible]	
	"	16	At [illegible], admitted a number of horses from [illegible] R.H.A., all of the animal being bad cases of debility, some of the worst have died.	
	"	17	Evacuated ninety sick horses today, more animals have died from debility and exhaustion during the night	
	"	18	At [illegible], visited units under my charge	
	"	19	Visited by A.D.V.S., arranging to evacuate about 90 sick animals tomorrow.	
	"	20	Evacuated 77 sick horses today — at [illegible].	
	"	21	N.C.O. in charge of conducting party on last evacuation, reports on return that a bad case of [illegible] occurred at Romescamps on the way down on Wednesday last, a number of sick horses were thrown off their feet in the trucks. [illegible] of conducting party injured and admitted to hospital. Have taken a written report from N.C.O. and am forwarding it to A.D.V.S.	
	"	22	A horse from 93 A.C. 3 [illegible] died from debility and exhaustion — at [illegible]	
	"	23	Visited units under my charge, visited by A.D.V.S. — at [illegible]	

2353 Wt. W2544/1454 700,000 5/15 D. D. & L. A.D.S.S./Forms/C. 2118.

Instructions regarding War Diaries and Intelligence Summaries are contained in F. S. Regs., Part II. and the Staff Manual respectively. Title pages will be prepared in manuscript.

WAR DIARY
or
INTELLIGENCE SUMMARY.
(Erase heading not required.)

Army Form C. 2118.

Place	Date	Hour	Summary of Events and Information	Remarks and references to Appendices
	1917 April	24	Evacuated 72 sick cases today. Had to destroy a horse with Fractured [illegible].	
	"	25	Destroyed a horse of the [illegible] Parks, [illegible] Engaged at Station	
	"	26	Visiting Units under my charge, Destroyed a case of [illegible] of [illegible] 22 RFA. — At Station, ADVS visited me	
	"	27	Evacuated 37 sick cases today, I have received instructions that I have to be prepared to hand over to [illegible] of my station horses.	
	"	28	The attached men of 22 [illegible] have had to be returned to their Units this week, If I have the same number of horses as I have had the past month, my men will not be sufficient to cope with them. [illegible] the attached men have been recalled — At Station.	
	"	29	Visiting Units under my charge, during the month a [illegible] have been attached for [illegible], that [illegible] have been treated & sent to [illegible]. I have received an intimation that the number of sick horses, [illegible], are to be immediately reduced by the	
	"	30	[illegible] to evacuate about six horses of [illegible] R.F.A. for sick horses, Visited by ADVS.	P.T.O.

J W Dawson

Capt AVC
O/C [illegible] Vety Section

2353 Wt. W2544/1454 700,000 5/15 D. D. & L. A.D.S.S./Forms/C. 2118.

Instructions regarding War Diaries and Intelligence Summaries are contained in F. S. Regs., Part II. and the Staff Manual respectively. Title pages will be prepared in manuscript.

WAR DIARY
or
INTELLIGENCE SUMMARY.
(Erase heading not required.)

Army Form C. 2118.

Place	Date	Hour	Summary of Events and Information	Remarks and references to Appendices
			During the month 513 sick horses have been admitted to the section. 398 have been evacuated to Base Vet. Hospitals 97 have died 14 have been destroyed and [illegible] have been returned cured.	
			G. H. Kinnear [illegible] Capt. A.V.C. O/C [illegible]	

2353 Wt. W2544/1454 700,000 5/15 D. D. & L. A.D.S.S./Forms/C. 2118.

Instructions regarding War Diaries and Intelligence Summaries are contained in F. S. Regs., Part II. and the Staff Manual respectively. Title pages will be prepared in manuscript.

WAR DIARY
or
INTELLIGENCE SUMMARY.
(Erase heading not required.)

Army Form C. 2118.

Vol 27

Place	Date	Hour	Summary of Events and Information	Remarks and references to Appendices
			Confidential	
			War Diary	
			of	
			Captain J. M. Dawson A.V.C.	
			o/c 12. Mobile Vety Section	
			7th Division.	
			1917 May 1st to 31st	

A7092' Wt. W128_9/M1293. 750,000. 1/17. D. D & I. Ltd. Forms/C2118/14.

Army Form C. 2118.

Instructions regarding War Diaries and Intelligence Summaries are contained in F. S. Regs., Part II. and the Staff Manual respectively. Title pages will be prepared in manuscript.

WAR DIARY
or
INTELLIGENCE SUMMARY.
(Erase heading not required.)

Place	Date	Hour	Summary of Events and Information	Remarks and references to Appendices
1917	May 1st		Evacuated Six sick horses to-day, have received an intimation that I have to send one NCO and three men from my Section to help form a Corps Mobile Veterinary Section further details of which I am to receive later, visited by A.D.V.S., latter expects to go on leave any day. I am to act as his deputy in his absence	
"	2nd		A.D.V.S went on leave this morning so take up temporary duty of A.D.V.S. Sent float to 11 M.D.A.C. for sick horse	
"	3rd		Arranging to evacuate four trucks of sick horses tomorrow, visited A.D.V.S office, at Section	
"	4th		Evacuated four trucks of horses to-day, visited units under my veterinary charge, at A.D.V.S office	
"	5th		Motored to MIRAMONT Railhead with D.A.Q.M.G. to inspect a number of remounts which came up from Base - afternoon - engaged afternoon at Section	
"	6th		At Section, and A.D.V.S office	
"	7th		Arranging to evacuate sick horses to-morrow, visiting units, at A.D.V.S. office	
"	8th		Evacuated 24 sick cases to-day.	
"	9th		At Section - visited units, A.D.V.S office	
"	10th		Had interview with Divisional Gas officer and arranging for a demonstration with new pattern Gas	

Instructions regarding War Diaries and Intelligence Summaries are contained in F. S. Regs., Part II. and the Staff Manual respectively. Title pages will be prepared in manuscript.

WAR DIARY
or
INTELLIGENCE SUMMARY.
(Erase heading not required.)

Army Form C. 2118.

Place	Date	Hour	Summary of Events and Information	Remarks and references to Appendices
1917	May		Helmet for Horses to be held at the Section on Tuesday next at 3 p.m.,	
	11th		At Section, and A D V S office	
	12th		Arranging with "G" Office to insert notice of Tuesday's demonstration in Divisional Routine Orders Visiting Units	
	13th		Engaged at Section, at A D V S office	
	14th		Arranging to evacuate 38 Sick Horses tomorrow, visited Units	
	15th		Evacuated Sick horses today 5 mules, Demonstration held this afternoon, a large attendance of Officers	
	16th		A D V S has returned from leave, at Section	
	17th		Visited Units under my charge, at Section	
	18th		Went on leave to England today	
	to 28		On leave	
	31		Arranging to evacuate 25 Sick cases tomorrow – at Section	
			During the month 197 Sick horses have been admitted 189 transferred to Hospital L of C and 19 returned cured. There has been no deaths in the Section and none of the cases admitted have been incurable – necessitating destruction, 31 Surplus animals have been dealt with during the month.	

J M Dawson
Capt AVC
O/C
12 Mobile Vet. Section

2353 Wt. W2544/1454 700,000 5/15 D. D. & L. A.D.S.S./Forms/C. 2118.

Instructions regarding War Diaries and Intelligence Summaries are contained in F. S. Regs., Part II. and the Staff Manual respectively. Title pages will be prepared in manuscript.

WAR DIARY

or

INTELLIGENCE SUMMARY.

(Erase heading not required.)

Army Form C. 2118.

Place	Date	Hour	Summary of Events and Information	Remarks and references to Appendices

A7092 Wt. W12S 9/M1293 750,000. 1/17. D. D & L. Ltd. Forms/C2118/14.

Instructions regarding War Diaries and Intelligence Summaries are contained in F. S. Regs., Part II. and the Staff Manual respectively. Title pages will be prepared in manuscript.

WAR DIARY
or
INTELLIGENCE SUMMARY.
(Erase heading not required.)

Army Form C. 2118.

Vol 28

Place	Date	Hour	Summary of Events and Information	Remarks and references to Appendices
			Confidential War Diary of Captain J. M. Dawson A.V.C. o/c 12. Mobile Section A.V.C. 7th Division. 1st June to 30th June 1917.	

A7092' Wt. W128.9/M1293 750,000. 1/17. D. D & L. Ltd. Forms/C2118/14.

Instructions regarding War Diaries and Intelligence Summaries are contained in F. S. Regs., Part II. and the Staff Manual respectively. Title pages will be prepared in manuscript.

WAR DIARY
or
INTELLIGENCE SUMMARY.
(Erase heading not required.)

Army Form C. 2118.

Place	Date	Hour	Summary of Events and Information	Remarks and references to Appendices
1917	June	1st	Evacuated 25 Sick horses today, at Station visited Units	
	"	2nd	Station and Units under my veterinary charge	
	"	3rd	Destroyed horse of 53 Batt RFA which had received a bad kick, Held Post Mortem examination of this animal and found that Bone has been fractured in one place	
	"	4th	Arranging to evacuate two trucks of sick horses tomorrow, taking over cases & deciding on hospital cases.	
	"	5th	Evacuated two trucks sick horses	
	"	6th	At Station, visiting Units	
	"	7th	Took over veterinary charge of 22 RFA Bde and 22nd Field Ambulance in absence of Captain Shell who is going on leave	
	"	8th	Visited Units named, preparing a weekly return (A 2000) for these units for A D V S	
	"	9th	Visited by A D V S, at Station	
	"	10th	Visited 22 RFA and Station	
	"	11th	Arranging to evacuate two trucks Sick Horses tomorrow, sorting over sick cases & deciding on hospital cases	
	"	12th	Evacuated two trucks Sick cases — Visited Units under my charge	

Army Form C. 2118.

Instructions regarding War Diaries and Intelligence Summaries are contained in F. S. Regs., Part II. and the Staff Manual respectively. Title pages will be prepared in manuscript.

WAR DIARY
or
INTELLIGENCE SUMMARY.
(*Erase heading not required.*)

Place	Date	Hour	Summary of Events and Information	Remarks and references to Appendices
1917	June	13th	Visited units 22 MFA & 22 Field Ambulance	
	"	14th	At Section, do not think it will be necessary to evacuate any cases tomorrow	
	"	15th	Did not evacuate to Hospital today, visited units, A D V S came to see me.	
	"	16th	Engaged at Section today	
	"	17th	At Section, visited units under my charge	
	"	18th	Am informed that A D V S is to be appointed A D V S [illegible] Corps and will be replaced in Division by a D A D V S	
	"	19th	Visited by A D V S. I have to take over duties of D A D V S until such appointment is made	
	"	20th	Looking over cases in Section and picking out cases for Hospital, visited units	
		21st	Arranging to evacuate seventeen cases tomorrow – At Section	
	"	22nd	Evacuated seventeen sick cases today, Understand I am to move to another area in a few days, Mobile [illegible] will move on 26th inst	
	"	23rd	Went to Railhead this morning to inspect Remounts which arrived from Base	
		24th	Arranging for Mobile to move tomorrow 25th, Rode up to new area to find suitable standings for horses, found a suitable spot near Behagnies where [illegible] are situated	

2353 Wt. W2544/1454 700,000 5/15 D. D. & L. A.D.S.S./Forms/C. 2118.

Army Form C. 2118.

WAR DIARY
or
INTELLIGENCE SUMMARY.
(Erase heading not required.)

Instructions regarding War Diaries and Intelligence Summaries are contained in F. S. Regs., Part II. and the Staff Manual respectively. Title pages will be prepared in manuscript.

Place	Date	Hour	Summary of Events and Information	Remarks and references to Appendices
1917	June	25th	Moved to new area this morning. Major [illegible] the newly appointed D.A.D.V.S. for the Division arrived at D.H.Q. today, visited me this afternoon and conferred with him.	
	"	26th	Visited by A.D.V.S. 3rd Corps, at Section.	
	"	27th	Engaged at Section, visited by D.A.D.V.S.	
	"	28th	Arranging to evacuate three trucks sick horses tomorrow, D.A.D.V.S. inspected sick cases.	
	"	29th	Evacuated 21 sick cases today, A.D.V.S. II Corps visited the Section, also D.A.D.V.S. held conference of V.O.s of Division this afternoon. All V.O.s were present.	
	"	30th	Engaged at Section, attending D.A.D.V.S. at D.H.Q. at his request to confer on matters.	
			The number of sick horses admitted during the month is 86. Transferred sick 98. Died 1, destroyed 4 and cured (and reissued) 16. A number of remounts and surplus horses and mules have passed through the Section during the month.	
			J. M. Dawson Capt A.V.C. O/C 4th Mobile Vet. Section 7th Division	
			In the Field 30/6/17	

Army Form C. 2118.

Instructions regarding War Diaries and Intelligence Summaries are contained in F. S. Regs., Part II. and the Staff Manual respectively. Title pages will be prepared in manuscript.

WAR DIARY

or

INTELLIGENCE SUMMARY.

(Erase heading not required.)

Place	Date	Hour	Summary of Events and Information	Remarks and references to Appendices

A7092 Wt. W128_9/M1293 750,000. 1/17. D. D & L. Ltd. Forms/C2118/14.

Instructions regarding War Diaries and Intelligence Summaries are contained in F. S. Regs., Part II. and the Staff Manual respectively. Title pages will be prepared in manuscript.

WAR DIARY
or
INTELLIGENCE SUMMARY.
(Erase heading not required.)

Army Form C. 2118.

Vol 29

Place	Date	Hour	Summary of Events and Information	Remarks and references to Appendices

Confidential.

War Diary

of

Captain J.M. Dawson. A.V.C.

12. Mobile Veterinary Section
7th Division.

From 1st July to 31st July 1917.

A7092 Wt. W123.9/M1293 750,000. 1/17. D. D & L. Ltd. Forms/C2118/14.

Instructions regarding War Diaries and Intelligence Summaries are contained in F. S. Regs., Part II. and the Staff Manual respectively. Title pages will be prepared in manuscript.

WAR DIARY
or
INTELLIGENCE SUMMARY.
(Erase heading not required.)

Army Form C. 2118.

Place	Date	Hour	Summary of Events and Information	Remarks and references to Appendices
	1917 July	1st	At Section, and visiting units	[illegible]
		2nd	Arranging to evacuate three trucks sick horses tomorrow, DADVS came over and inspected cases which I prepared to send down	[illegible]
		3rd	Evacuated twenty three cases, visited units under my charge	[illegible]
	"	4th	At Section and units. Destroyed a horse of 35 Batt 22 RFA. Shot [illegible]	[illegible]
		5th	Went to 35 Bde RFA with DADVS and inspected the horses of the Brigade. At Section, arranged to evacuate four trucks of horses tomorrow, [illegible] cases to go. DADVS subsequently inspected these animals. [illegible]	[illegible]
	"	6th	Evacuated 27 sick cases today, went to railhead to see animals [illegible] [illegible] Field [illegible]	[illegible]
	"	7th	Visiting units and at Section	[illegible]
	"	8th	At Section and units	[illegible]
	"	9th	Arranging to evacuate sick horses tomorrow, DADVS inspected cases which I proposed to send. Destroyed a horse of 12 Batt 35 RFA, [illegible].	[illegible]
	"	10th	Evacuated 23 sick cases today	
	"	11th	At Section, visiting units under my vety charge.	[illegible]

2353 Wt. W2544/1454 700,000 5/15 D. D. & L. A.D.S.S./Forms/C. 2118.

Instructions regarding War Diaries and Intelligence Summaries are contained in F. S. Regs., Part II. and the Staff Manual respectively. Title pages will be prepared in manuscript.

WAR DIARY

or

INTELLIGENCE SUMMARY.

(Erase heading not required.)

Army Form C. 2118.

Place	Date	Hour	Summary of Events and Information	Remarks and references to Appendices
1917 July	12th		Arranging to Evacuate sick horses tomorrow, DADVS came over and inspected the cases	[illegible]
"	13th		Evacuated twenty six cases today, visiting units	[illegible]
"	14th		DDVS [illegible] came with DADVS and inspected animals sent in by [illegible] units which it was proposed to cast, picked out a number for casting	[illegible]
"	15th		At Section, visiting units under my charge	[illegible]
"	16th		Arranging to evacuate a number of sick cases tomorrow, about 50 change cases have been sent in to the Section today. Destroyed a horse of 5 A.R.E. [illegible] by [illegible]	[illegible]
"	17th		Evacuated seventy sick cases this morning, also [illegible] cases cast by DDVS [illegible]	[illegible]
"	18th		Visited units under my charge. Destroyed a horse of 112 [illegible] Batty R.G.A. [illegible]	[illegible]
"	19th		Arranging to again evacuate sick horses tomorrow, DADVS inspected cases	[illegible]
"	20th		Evacuated 25 sick cases today, also three mules cast by DDR, office & [illegible]	[illegible]
"	21st		Visited units and at Section today. Destroyed a horse of [illegible] [illegible]	[illegible]
"	22nd		Engaged at Section visiting units	[illegible]
"	23rd		Visiting units, at Section, arranging to evacuate sick horses tomorrow, DADVS inspected cases	[illegible]

2353 Wt. W2544/1454 700,000 5/15 D. D. & L. A.D.S.S./Forms/C. 2118.

Instructions regarding War Diaries and Intelligence Summaries are contained in F. S. Regs., Part II. and the Staff Manual respectively. Title pages will be prepared in manuscript.

WAR DIARY
or
INTELLIGENCE SUMMARY.
(*Erase heading not required.*)

Army Form C. 2118.

Place	Date	Hour	Summary of Events and Information	Remarks and references to Appendices
1917 July	24th		Evacuated three [illegible] sick horses today also three horses of 283 A F A Bde [illegible] Visited 21st and 22nd Infy Bdes, DADVS came to Section	[illegible]
"	25th		At Section, Visited units under my Vety Charge, arranging as to putting down standings for [illegible]	[illegible]
"	26th		Arranging to evacuate 24 sick cases tomorrow DADVS visited Section and inspected animals which I proposed to send away to Hospital. Visited units, office returns	[illegible]
"	27th		Evacuated 24 sick cases today, visiting units	
"	28th		Visiting units and at Section	[illegible]
"	29th		At Section Visiting units, Destroyed a horse of 12 Batty 35 RFA admitted with [illegible] fractured [illegible]	[illegible]
"	30th		Sent [illegible] for horse of 9th [illegible] from [illegible] — at Section	[illegible]
"	31st		Visited units, at Section	[illegible]
			During the month 272 cases have been admitted to the Section 239 cases have been evacuated to Base Hospital, six animals have been destroyed one died and 17 have been returned cured. A number of surplus animals from units in the Division and cases for casting have also been dealt with	

In the Field.

J. M. Dawson [illegible]
Capt AVC
O/C 12 [illegible] Section

2353 Wt. W2544/1454 700,000 5/15 D. D. & L. A.D.S.S./Forms/C. 2118.

Vol 30.

WAR DIARY

No 12 Mobile Vety Section

Vol 37.

Army Form C. 2118.

Instructions regarding War Diaries and Intelligence Summaries are contained in F. S. Regs., Part II. and the Staff Manual respectively. Title pages will be prepared in manuscript.

WAR DIARY
or
~~INTELLIGENCE SUMMARY.~~ No 12 Mobile Vety Section

(Erase heading not required.)

Place	Date	Hour	Summary of Events and Information	Remarks and references to Appendices
BEHAGNIES Aug	1	1917	Usual Office Routine	
Thur	2		DADVS visited Section. Staff Sergeant SE 886 KNOWLER proceeded on leave	
Fri	3		Evacuated 22 sick horses to No 7 Vety Hospital FORGES LES EAUX from ACHIET LEGRAND Station	
Sat	4		Usual Office Routine	
Sun	5		Usual Office Routine	
Mon	6		DADVS visited Section & inspected sick horses	
Tue	7		DADVS visited Section & inspected some Mange cases sent to the Section for that purpose	
Wed	8		SE 554 Sergeant BOULDTHORPE, SE 2991 Private BUCHAN & SE 4416 Private NUTTER proceeded on leave	
Thurs	9		DADVS visited Section & inspected sick horses	
Fri	10		Evacuated 34 sick horses. Section moved at 1 pm & reached camp in BRETENCOURT at 4 pm.	
BRETENCOURT (RIVIERE) Sat	11		Section employed arranging camp & lines	
Sun	12		Usual Office Routine	

A7092 Wt. W128 9/M1293 750,000. 1/17. D. D & I. Ltd. Forms/C2118/14.

Instructions regarding War Diaries and Intelligence Summaries are contained in F. S. Regs., Part II. and the Staff Manual respectively. Title pages will be prepared in manuscript.

WAR DIARY
or
~~INTELLIGENCE~~ SUMMARY. No. 12 Mobile Vety Section

(*Erase heading not required.*)

Army Form C. 2118.

Place	Date	Hour	Summary of Events and Information	Remarks and references to Appendices
BRETENCOURT (RIVIERE) Mon	13	1917	Section Float went to 7 DAC & collected 1 horse	
Tue	14		A number of Surplus Horses received at Section. Result of reduction in Establishment. Several Officers deficient of Chargers inspected the animals in accordance with D.R.O. No 652.	
Wed	15		Usual Office Routine	
Thurs	16		Usual Office Routine.	
Fri	17		SE 3984 Cpl DAVIS. T promoted to P/a Sergeant from 14-8-17 and SE 3410 Private WHITE. F promoted to P/A Corporal from 20/7/17 in accordance with Local Corps Orders 69.	
Sat	18		SE 718 Private SCRASE. A and 32961 Pte REDDINGS. proceeded on leave	
Sun	19		Usual Office Routine	
Mon	20		Usual Office Routine.	

Instructions regarding War Diaries and Intelligence Summaries are contained in F. S. Regs., Part II. and the Staff Manual respectively. Title pages will be prepared in manuscript.

WAR DIARY
or
~~INTELLIGENCE SUMMARY.~~ No. 12 Mobile Vety. Section

(Erase heading not required.)

Army Form C. 2118.

Place	Date	Hour	Summary of Events and Information	Remarks and references to Appendices
BRETENCOURT (RIVIERE)				
Tue	21	1917	R.A. Section, Base, notifies us that Driver ASTLE. 230 R.F.A. attached to this Section & at present on leave, would receive his discharge in England & that he was to be struck of strength of unit	
Wed	22		Evacuated 14 sick horses to day to No 7 Vety Hospital. FORGES LES EAUX. from Exeter Station	
Thurs	23		P/A Sergeant DAVIS No SE 3984 departed for No 23 Vety Hospital. ST. OMER & was struck off the strength of this Section. Two A.V.C privates wired for to A.V.C Records to complete Establishment.	
Fri	24		SE 13799 Private MEAD. W. proceeded to England on account of his application for temporary commission in A.S.C & was struck off strength of Section.	
Sat	25.		Captain DAWSON proceeded on leave, Captain BRAID took over charge of Section	
	"		N.C.O. and nine men of Section on police duty at Divisional Fair at HENDECOURT. PB.	
Sund	26		D.A.D.V.S. visited Section. PB	
Mon	27		Smoke Helmet Drill. PB.	

2353 Wt. W2544/1454 700,000 5/15 D. D. & L. A.D.S.S./Forms/C. 2118.

Instructions regarding War Diaries and Intelligence Summaries are contained in F. S. Regs., Part II. and the Staff Manual respectively. Title pages will be prepared in manuscript.

WAR DIARY
or
~~INTELLIGENCE SUMMARY.~~
(Erase heading not required.)

No. 12 Mobile Vety Section

Army Form C. 2118.

Place	Date	Hour	Summary of Events and Information	Remarks and references to Appendices
BRETENCOURT (RIVIERE)				
Tue	28	1917	Evacuated seven sick horses to 23 M.V.S. ACHICOURT. PB	
Wed	29		Evacuated two sick horses to 23 M.V.S. ACHICOURT. PB	
Thurs	30		Section moved to RENINGHELST. Left BRETENCOURT at 4.15 a.m. Arrived at SAULTY at 7.30 am. where we entrained from. Watered horses before leaving. Reached DOULLENS at 12.30 pm where we watered + fed. Reached HAZEBROUCK at 4.30 pm where we again water + fed. Arrived at PROVEN at 9.30 pm where we detrained + tracked to our destination at RENINGHELST. PB	
Friday	31		Arrived RENINGHELST at 2 am + found camp very unsatisfactory. Made arrangements with Area Commandant to move Section to another position. PB	

P. Brand Capt. AVC
O/C 12 M.V.S.

A7092 Wt. W128.9/M1293 750,000. 1/17. D. D & L. Ltd. Forms/C2118/14.

Vol 31

WAR DIARY.

12th Mobile Veterinary Section. September 1917

D.A.D.V.S.,
7th DIVISION.
No. ....
Date ....

Instructions regarding War Diaries and Intelligence Summaries are contained in F. S. Regs., Part II. and the Staff Manual respectively. Title pages will be prepared in manuscript.

WAR DIARY
or
INTELLIGENCE SUMMARY.
(*Erase heading not required.*)

No. 12 MOBILE VETERINARY SECTION.
No. ....
Date ....

Volume 38

Army Form C. 2118.

Place	Date	Hour	Summary of Events and Information	Remarks and references to Appendices
RENINGHELST	1-9-17		Section moved about five hundred yards to a place more suitable for sick horses. D.A.D.V.S visited Section & gave orders for Section to move with 91 Inf Bde to STEENVOORDE. left RENINGHELST at 5 30 pm & reached our destination without mishap at 10-30 pm. & camped for the night.	
			SE10907 Pte SHARP proceeded on leave to England from 2/9/17 to 12/9/17	
STEENVOORDE	2 9 17		Section had orders to be ready to move at short notice.	
			32961 Dr. REDDINGS returned from leave	
"	3/9/17		Bombs fell on this village this morning. Section left STEENVOORDE at 2.20 pm & reached HONDEGHEM at 6-15 pm. Obtained good billets. Orderly sent to 91 Inf Bde Hd Qrs.	
HONDEGHEM	4-9-17		Usual Office Routine, No SE 230 Private ALLEN and No SE 8462 Private HAWTIN reported here for duty from No 2 Veterinary Hospital LE HAVRE.	
	5-9-17		D.A.D.V.S. visited Section. Collected five Remounts from Remount Depot LE BREARDE.	
			Captain DAWSON returned from leave.	
	6-9-17		D.ADVS. visited Section.	
	7-9-17		Usual Office Routine.	
	8-9-17		No SE 406 Private WILSHER proceeded on leave to England.	
	9/9/17		Usual Office Routine.	

A7092. Wt. W128 9/M1293. 750,000. 1/17. D. D & L. Ltd. Forms/C2118/14.

Instructions regarding War Diaries and Intelligence Summaries are contained in F. S. Regs., Part II. and the Staff Manual respectively. Title pages will be prepared in manuscript.

WAR DIARY
or
INTELLIGENCE SUMMARY.
(Erase heading not required.)

No. 12 MOBILE VETERINARY SECTION.
No.........
Date.........

Army Form C. 2118.

Volume 38

Place	Date	Hour	Summary of Events and Information	Remarks and references to Appendices
HONDEGHEM	10/9/17		Collected 2 horses of 7 F Aus. B. at STAPLES	GMD
	11-9-17		DADVS visited Section. Collected ten remounts from BAILLEUL	GMD
	12-9-17		D.A.D.V.S visited Section	GMD
	13-9-17		Collected two horses from 6 Aus Bde EECKE. Section moved at 2 pm + arrived at ARQUES at 5 pm. Four horses evacuated to 23 Vety Hospital, ST OMER, by motor ambulance. Two horses left at No 8 Sick Halt.	GMD
ARQUES	14-9-17		Evacuated 15 horses + two mules to 23 Vety Hospital ST OMER.	GMD
	15-9-17		No SE Private FRANCIS proceeded on leave to England. Section moved at 2 pm + arrived at WIZERNES at 3-30 pm.	GMD
WIZERNES.	16-9-17		No. SE 10907 Private SHARP returned from leave.	GMD
	17-9-17		Usual Office Routine.	GMD
	18-9-17		SE 2465 Private T. COX proceeded on Special leave to England from 19/9/17 to 2/10/17	GMD
	19/9/17		Evacuated seven horses to 23 Vety Hospital ST OMER.	GMD
	20/9/17		SE 406 Private WILSHER returned from leave.	GMD
	21/9/17		Evacuated twenty three horses and two mules to 23rd Vety Hospital ST. OMER.	GMD

A7092 Wt. W128.9/M1293. 750,000. 1/17. D. D & L. Ltd. Forms/C2118/14.

Instructions regarding War Diaries and Intelligence Summaries are contained in F. S. Regs., Part II. and the Staff Manual respectively. Title pages will be prepared in manuscript.

WAR DIARY
or
INTELLIGENCE SUMMARY.
(Erase heading not required.)

Army Form C. 2118.

No. 12 MOBILE VETERINARY SECTION. No. .... Date ....

Volume 38

Place	Date	Hour	Summary of Events and Information	Remarks and references to Appendices
WIZERNES	22/9/17		Usual Office Rountine	GMD
	23/9/17		Usual Office Routine.	GMD
	24/9/17		SE No 3410 Corporal WHITE and SE No. 406 Private WILSHER proceeded to establish Veterinary Aid Post on Divisional Manouvres.	GMD
	25/9/17		No SE 512 Cpl KNOWLER and No SE 1129 Private WATTS. proceeded on leave to England.	GMD
	26/9/17		Usual Office Routine	GMD
	27/9/17		Evacuated seven horses and one mule to 23rd Vety Hospital St OMER	GMD
	28/9/17		Section moved at 8-30 am + arrived at HONDEGHEM at 5pm and camped there for the night.	GMD
HONDEGHEM	29/9/17		Section moved off again at 7 a.m. + reached WESTOUTRE at 5.30 pm where we camped for the night to await further orders. DADVS returned from leave.	GMD
WESTOUTRE	30/9/17		Usual Office Routine.	GMD

G M Dawson
Capt AVC
O/C. 12th Mobile Vety Section

A7092 Wt. W128.9/M1293. 750,000. 1/17. D. D & L. Ltd. Forms/C2118/14.

WAR DIARY

12 Mob Vety Section

VOL 38.

No. 12 MOBILE VETERINARY SECTION
Army Form C. 2118.
No.
Date

Instructions regarding War Diaries and Intelligence Summaries are contained in F. S. Regs., Part II. and the Staff Manual respectively. Title pages will be prepared in manuscript.

WAR DIARY
or
~~INTELLIGENCE SUMMARY.~~
(Erase heading not required.)

Volume 39

Place	Date	Hour	Summary of Events and Information	Remarks and references to Appendices
WESTOUTRE	1/10/17		Section moved at 11 am and arrived at LA CLYTTE at 1 15 pm. DADVS visited Section	[initials] [initials]
LA.CLYTTE	2/10/17		D A D.V.S visited Section	
	3/10/17		Corporal WHITE and two men proceeded to 1. 19. b. 7.5. Sheet 27 to form Advanced Veterinary Aid Post	[initials] [initials]
	4/10/17		Usual Office Routine. SE 2465 Pte COX. J. returned from leave to England	[initials]
	5/10/17		Evacuated thirty seven horses and thirteen mules to No 13 Veterinary Hospital through Casualty Clearing Section at WIPPENHOEK.	
	6/10/17		Usual Office Routine. No SE 10857 Pte ~~Hughes~~ HUGHES admitted to No 11 Casualty Clearing Station	[initials]
	7/10/17		D. A. D. V. S. visited Section	[initials]
	8/10/17		Section moved a few hundred yards to a more suitable place for sick horses. Took over sixteen sick horses from outgoing M.V.S No 28.	[initials]
	9/10/17		Usual Routine Office.	

A7092 Wt. W128.9/M1293. 750,000. 1/17. D. D & L. Ltd. Forms/C2118/14.

Instructions regarding War Diaries and Intelligence Summaries are contained in F. S. Regs., Part II. and the Staff Manual respectively. Title pages will be prepared in manuscript.

WAR DIARY
or
~~INTELLIGENCE SUMMARY.~~
(Erase heading not required.)

No. 12
MOBILE VETERINARY SECTION.
No.........
Date.........

Army Form C. 2118.

Volume 39

Place	Date	Hour	Summary of Events and Information	Remarks and references to Appendices
LA CLYTTE.	10/10/17		D.A.D.V.S visited Section. No ~~SE Sgt~~ 554 Sgt GOULDTHORPE reported at Casualty Clearing Section OUDERDOM for duty.	gmw
	11/10/17		Evacuated Sixty six horses and sixteen mules to Casualty Clearing Section at OUDERDOM No SE 512 Corporal KNOWLER, returned from leave to England.	gmw
	12/10/17		Section moved at 4 pm and arrived at BERTHEN about 6-30 pm where we camped. No SE 8462 Pte HAWTIN and 1554 Dr HODGSON. RFA reported for duty to Casualty Clearing Section at OUDERDOM.	gmw
			No SE 512 Corporal KNOWLER and six men left with 23rd Divisional Mobile Vety Section at LA CLYTTE for duty. No SE 3410 Cpl WHITE and two men withdrawn from advance post at I 19 b 7.5	
BERTHEN.	13/10/17		Twelve men arrived at Section to relieve twelve section men who have been classed as category 'A' + who are to report as soon as possible at No 2 Veterinary Hospital LE HAVRE.	gmw
	14/10/17		Six men under charge of Cpl KNOWLER who remained at LA CLYTTE with 23rd Divisional Mobile were recalled and replaced by six more men from Section.	gmw
	15/10/17		Ten men from Section classed as category 'A' proceeded to No 2 Veterinary Hospital LE HAVRE per instructions of Officer i/c AVC Base Records, 14/1654/17 dated 7/10/17.	gmw
			Two men left Section to report to O.C. Casualty Clearing Section OUDERDOM and replace two men sent there on 12/10/17	gmw
	16.10.17.		SE. 2452. Sgt Brookes. F. granted leave to England for 10 dys. from 16.10.17 to 26.10.17.	gmw

A7092 Wt. W128 9/M1293. 750,000. 1/17. D. D & I. Ltd. Forms/C2118/14.

Instructions regarding War Diaries and Intelligence Summaries are contained in F. S. Regs., Part II. and the Staff Manual respectively. Title pages will be prepared in manuscript.

WAR DIARY
or
~~INTELLIGENCE SUMMARY.~~
(*Erase heading not required.*)

Army Form C. 2118.

No. 12 MOBILE VETERI[NARY] SECTION.
No. ....
Date ....

Volume ...

Place	Date	Hour	Summary of Events and Information	Remarks and references to Appendices
Berthen	17.10.17		S.E. 10907. Pte Sharp F. W. proceeded to No 2 Vet. Hospital Le Havre	G.M.D.
	18.10.17		Usual Office Routine.	G.M.D.
	19.10.17		Collected float case from A. 52 Bde: R.F.A.	G.M.D.
	20.10.17		Collected 2. strays from M Degrave near Becke. D.A.D.V.S. visited section & issued out 12 remounts which arrived same day. 1. (One) floatcase sent to 10. Corps Vet: C.C.S.	G.M.D.
	21.10.17		Collected 1. (one) horse left with M Leon Deguchet of float case sent to 2nd Anzac Corps (R.H.T. Rule)	G.M.D.
	22.10.17		Leave destinations for Cpl. Richards & Pte Bounds sent in to A.D.V.S.	G.M.D.
	23.10.17		Lymphangitis remount floated to C.C.S. 2nd Anzac Corps.	G.M.D.
Westoutre	24.10.17		Section left Berthen about 11 a. arrived Westoutre about 12 noon: D.A.D.V.S. visited Section. took over Celulitis case from 5th M.V.S. Off wheel of Canadian Waggon collapsed. Float case sent to 10. Corps C.C.S. Sgt. Goldthorpe promoted Staff Sergt. Local Corps order No 71.	G.M.D.
	25.10.17		Clipped A.D.V.S. two chargers. D.A.D.V.S. visited Section. Corporal Knowles & six men & four horses rejoined Section from 33rd M.V.S. Staff/Sgt. went Caestre to take descriptions. Indented for Limber to replace smashed waggon. Post issued from 20th Bde dump. Corporal White went to collect horse from D.15.b.3.7 but found had already been collected by Ambulance.	G.M.D.

A7092. Wt. W128 9/M1293 750,000. 1/17. D. D & L. Ltd. Forms/C2118/14.

Instructions regarding War Diaries and Intelligence Summaries are contained in F. S. Regs., Part II. and the Staff Manual respectively. Title pages will be prepared in manuscript.

WAR DIARY
or
~~INTELLIGENCE SUMMARY.~~
(Erase heading not required.)

No. 12 MOBILE VETERINARY SECTION. No. ... Date ... Volume 39

Army Form C. 2118.

Place	Date	Hour	Summary of Events and Information	Remarks and references to Appendices
Westoutre	26.X.17		Evacuated 17 Horses & 2 Mules to 23rd V.H. Cpl. White i/c & 3 men. 9 of which were collected from the 2nd Field Remount Section II Army. rained all day	JMD
	27.X.17		D.A.D.V.S. visited Section. Pt. Bounds left with 2 men for the 2nd Field Remount Section II Army to help fetch remounts back tomorrow. 4 men from the 21st Divisional Employment Co. reported this morn.	JMD
	28.X.17		Cpl. White & Pt. Bounds returned with 44 remounts. D.A.D.V.S. called. Paid out.	JMD
	29.X.17		Evacuated 10 Horses 2 Mules to Vety. C.C.S. 10 Corps. Issued remounts. 4 men from 21st Div. Employment Co. left.	JMD
Blaringhem	30.X.17		Section left Westoutre about 9.30 a.m. arrived Blaringhem about 5.30. Wet day. Sgt. Brookes returned from leave.	JMD
	31.X.17		D.A.D.V.S. visited Section. Sgt. Cossey arrived from No 2 Hospital.	JMD

J M Dawson Capt. AVC

Vol 33

12 Mob Vety Section

WAR DIARY

VOLUME No. 39

Instructions regarding War Diaries and Intelligence Summaries are contained in F. S. Regs., Part II. and the Staff Manual respectively. Title pages will be prepared in manuscript.

WAR DIARY
or
INTELLIGENCE SUMMARY.
(*Erase heading not required.*)

Army Form C. 2118.

No. 12 MOBILE VETERINARY SECTION
No. ....
Date 5.5.17

Volume 40.

Place	Date	Hour	Summary of Events and Information	Remarks and references to Appendices
Racquinghem	1.11.17		Section left Blaringhem @ 9oc. arrived Racquinghem 10 oc	Gud
	2.11.17		Evacuated 10 horses to 23rd Vety Hosp. Cpl White i/c of 2 men. Corporal Knowler & 2 men proceeded to Dickebush to collect 13 Animals cast by D.D.R. Returned G.S. waggon borrowed from 1C Team.	Gud
	3.11.17		D.A.D.V.S. visited Section. Started clipping.	Gud
	4.11.17		Clipping. Buried 2 horses. Smith called. Gibson reported sick	Gud
	5.11.17		Usual office routine	Gud
	6.11.17		Evacuated 12 Horses to No. 23 V.H. Cpl White i/c. D.A.D.V.S. called	Gud
	7.11.17		Capt. Richards left for 14 days leave.	Gud
	8.11.17		Usual office routine.	Gud
	9.11.17		Usual office routine.	Gud
	10.11.17		Evacuated 4 horses (1 float case) & 2 mules to No. 23 V.H. Cpl. Knowler i/c.	Gud
	11.11.17		Usual Office Routine	Gud
	12.11.17		Section left Racquinghem @ 10 a.m. arrived Provendaal 5.00 p.m.	Gud
	13.11.17		D.A.D.V.S. visited Section. 1 G.S. Waggon left 3.0 pm Sgt Cowser i/c to draw rations @ Ypres joining us @ Dongeval on the following day. Cpl. Knowler & two men left for No. 4 Remount Depot. To collect 25 remounts	Gud

A6945 Wt. W11422/M1160 350,000 12/16 D. D. & L. Forms/C./2118/14.

Instructions regarding War Diaries and Intelligence Summaries are contained in F. S. Regs., Part II. and the Staff Manual respectively. Title pages will be prepared in manuscript.

WAR DIARY
or
INTELLIGENCE SUMMARY.
(Erase heading not required.)

Army Form C. 2118.

No. 12 MOBILE VETERINARY SECTION. Date 5.12.17

Volume 40

Place	Date	Hour	Summary of Events and Information	Remarks and references to Appendices
Boyaval	14.11.17		Left Pravendaal 9.30 arrived Boyaval @ 5.30 p.m.	gwd
	15.11.17		Pte Hawtin & Hodgson returned from V.C.C.S 10 Corps.	gwd
	16.11.17		Cpl Knowles left with men to collect remounts	gwd
	17.11.17		Evacuated 11 horses to Hesdin @ Sick Horse Halt	gwd
Warrans	18.11.17		The Section left Boyaval @ 3.30 arrived Warrans 6.30 pm left behind 1 L.D. from 528 Field Co Durham R.E. Dutton	gwd
	19.11.17		The Section entrained for Italy @ 8.30. left behind 3 H.D. 2 from 2nd Gordons Blind. 1 from 3 Coy Div Trn. dropped sale N.F. (Foot case)	gwd
Legnago	26.11.17		Arrived ~~Legnana~~ LEGNAGO 6.30 a.m. detrained, picketed in a field adjoining station moved into Billett @ 4 oc. Cpl Richards returned from leave.	gwd
Pojana	27.11.17		Left Legnago 9.30 a.m. arrived Pojana 3.30. left Staff Sgt Knowles Pte Rimmalls, Hawtin & Cpl Parsons behind	gwd
Albettone	28.11.17		Left ~~Legnago~~ Pojana 9.30 arrived Albettone 3 oc. Captain Dawson returned to Lignagna	gwd
	29.11.17		Capt Dawson Staff Sgt Knowles Pte Hawtin rejoined Section Cpl Parsons & Pte Rimmals left Lignagna by rail with sick horses for Pavia	gwd
	30.11.17		Cpl Richards & Pte Holt proceeded to Lugacchi to collect 2 sick horses	gwd

GWDawson Capt AVC

A7092 Wt. W128/M1293. 750,000. 1/17. D. D & L. Ltd. Forms/C2118/14.

www.ingramcontent.com/pod-product-compliance
Lightning Source LLC
Chambersburg PA
CBHW081410160426
43193CB00013B/2146